Obituaries, Death Notices, and Genealogical Gleanings from The Saugerties Telegraph Volume 1: 1848-1852

A family and Business Newspaper;
Neutral in Politics; Devoted to Literature,
Morality, Foreign and Domestic News,
Education, Agriculture, Science,
Art and Amusement

Volume 1: 1848-1852

Audrey M. Klinkenberg

HERITAGE BOOKS
2008

HERITAGE BOOKS

AN IMPRINT OF HERITAGE BOOKS, INC.

Books, CDs, and more—Worldwide

For our listing of thousands of titles see our website
at
www.HeritageBooks.com

Published 2008 by
HERITAGE BOOKS, INC.
Publishing Division
100 Railroad Ave. #104
Westminster, Maryland 21157

Copyright © 1989 Audrey M. Klinkenberg

Other books by the author:

Marriages from The Saugerties Telegraph 1846-1870 and Obituaries, Death Notices and Genealogical Gleanings from The Ulster Telegraph 1846-1848
Obituaries, Death Notices, and Genealogical Gleanings from The Saugerties Telegraph, Volume 2: 1853-1860
Obituaries, Death Notices, and Genealogical Gleanings from The Saugerties Telegraph, Volume 3: 1861-1870
Obituaries, Death Notices & Genealogical Gleanings from the Saugerties Telegraph, Volume 4 1871-1879
Obituaries, Death Notices & Genealogical Gleanings from the Saugerties Telegraph, Volume 5: 1880-1884
CD: New York: Volume 5, Obituaries, Death Notices and Genealogical Gleanings from The Saugerties Telegraph, Volumes 1-3

International Standard Book Numbers
Paperbound: 978-1-55613-252-0
Clothbound: 978-0-7884-7064-6

INTRODUCTION

Saugerties, Ulster County, New York, a town on the Hudson River, about one hundred miles north of New York City, published an early newspaper, The Ulster _Telegraph_, in 1846. By 1851 the name had changed to The Saugerties _Telegraph_. Publication continued through the early 1950's.

Bound volumes of the newspaper 1848-1884 were preserved by the local library. With the miracle of modern technology these papers have been microfilmed and are readily accessible to the researcher.

I have carefully read each available newspaper, in its original form, abstracting notices of death and copying various items of genealogical interest along the way. I am perpetually amazed by the scope of news presented 140 years ago in this small town weekly. On some days more time was spent reading articles than on gathering the data for this volume.

Small steps in genealogical research lead the seeker on the right path. If one small step in this book helps to extend or clarify a family line, I will be satisified.

Audrey M. Klinkenberg
Saugerties, New York

NEWSPAPER ABSTRACTS

December 30, 1848
1. Monday last, in this town, John L. Wynkoop, about 40.

2. Sunday morning, Chelsea, Mass., Mr. William Snelling, editor of the Boston Herald, aged 44.

3. Sunday morning, Chelsea, Mass., Mr. Simon Jordon, father-in-law of Mr. William Snelling, aged 65.

4. Thursday last, Pughtown, Brooke Co., Va., Mr. White, a suicide, leaving a wife and children. (Pittsburgh Post).

5. Charles Mc Vean, Esq., United States District Attorney for the Southern District of New York, died on the 28th inst., aged 46 years and 2 months. Born in Johnstown, NY. (True Sun).

6. The funeral of Hon. James A. Black, late member of Congress from South Carolina, took place at Columbia, SC on the 19th inst.

7. Friday, on the corner of Henry and Walnut streets in New York, Francis Geiger and Mr. Marks killed each other over a woman named Maria Kloster. (NY Sunday Times).

January 6, 1849
8. Monday last, in this village, Mr. John W. Hays, about 64.

9. Thursday last, in this village, George Washington, son of Curtis Hoyt, aged 1 year and 4 months.

10. Peter C. Brooks, the wealthiest man in New England, died on Monday night at his residence in Melford, aged about 84. He was the father-in-law of Edward Everett, Rev. Mr. Frothingham and Charles Francis Adams, and president of the Massachusetts Life Insurance Co. (Boston Post).

January 13, 1849

11. Hon. Ambrose H. Sevier, of Arkansas, died on
the 1st instant

January 20, 1849

12. Friday, in this village, Mrs. Leah Mynderse,
about 71.

13. Jan 6, Groveland, Michigan, Rev. David
Webster, formerly of this village.

14. The son of John Wells, deceased, aged 7, slid
into a team of horses and was killed. (Whitehall
Chronicle).

15. Sunday last, a lad named Roberts was killed.
(Westchester Herald).

16. Last evening, Charles Cushen, about 20, an
Englishman, was hit by a train. (Springfield
Republican).

17. Gen. Rutland, of St. Louis, one of Gen.
Harrison's aids and a long time Indian Agent, died
at Jefferson City, Missouri on the fifth.

18. Col. Croghan, Inspector General of the Army,
died at Washington on Saturday.

19. Col. Dix died at Hillsboro and Major Miller
died at Brownville, probably of Asiatic cholera,
on Sunday last. (Wheeling Times of the 11th
inst.).

20. An inquest was held yesterday on the body of
Christopher Davis, a native of NY, aged 60, who
died by being run over by the Croton train on the
NY and Harlem Railroad at 4th avenue and 42nd
street. (True Sun of Tuesday).

January 27, 1849

21. Monday last, Poughkeepsie, Edward H. Davis,
aged 28, formerly of Kingston.

22. Jan 8, Kingston, Sarah, widow of Thomas Van
Bramer, aged 73.

23. On the 4th inst., frozen to death near his
home, Mr. John Harvey of Jefferson, Me. (Augusta
Age).

24. Friday last, at Castleton, Miss Sarah Crehore died from hydrophobia. She was a member of the Handel and Haydn Society. (Boston Transcript).

25. Tuesday, Wilmington, Del., Dr. John Lofland, one of the editors of the Blue Hen's Chicken.

26. Mr. David Hale, one of the editors of the New York Journal of Commerce died at Fredericksburgh on Sunday last.

27. Augustus F. Ives, youngest son of Chauncy Ives, Esq., of this village, shot himself accidently on Dec 20th in the town of Brownsville, Cameron county, Texas. He died 48 hours later. His brother, Oscar Ives died at Galveston, Texas of a fever. (Lansingburgh Democrat).

February 3, 1849
28. Saturday last, in this village, Mr. Benjamin F. Miller, in his 49th year.

29. On the 16th inst., Lewis County, Parsons Talcott, aged 60, was struck and killed by a falling tree, leaving relatives in Rome and Verona. (Utica Ob.).

30. Charles M. Clayton, son of Senator John M. Clayton of Delaware, died at Havana on the 20th inst., of pulmonary consumption.

31. Saturday night last, Mr. John Buckley, harness maker, was frozen to death, leaving a wife and two children. (Chicago Democrat).

32. Friday last, Port Stanley, Mr. George Bostwick murdered his wife, then cut his own throat. (Ham. (West Canada) Gaz.).

33. Burlington, Vt., on the 20th inst., James Dean, L. L. D., aged 73.

34. James Crocker of Bath, Maine, aged about 14 years, was drowned on Saturday evening while skating.

35. Andreas Hall, convicted on Friday at Troy of the murder of Mrs. Amy Smith, of Petersburgh, in July last, was sentenced to be hung on the 15th of March next. Barney O'Donnell was also sentenced to be hung on the same day, for the murder of Antonio Ratto.

3

February 10, 1849

36. On the 30th ult., in this village, Mrs. Elizabeth, wife of John H. Coon, aged 56.

37. Feb 2, in this town, Amelia G., wife of Wesley Lewis, and eldest daughter of Joseph Mount, Esq., in her 25th year.

38. On the 30th ult., New Baltimore, Harrid Wells, about 60, a blacksmith. (Catskill Democrat).

39. Mr. Benjamin Crane, whose family reside in Bloomingburgh, Sullivan County, was instantly killed Jan 22, by the unexpected discharge of a blast, on the Hudson River Rail road opposite West Point.

40. Samuel Frost, of the town of Pleasant Valley, Dutchess county was found dead in his bed a few mornings since. Cause of death unknown.

41. Samuel Jenkins, colored, 115 years old, died at Lancaster, Ohio on Jan 4. He was born a slave in Fairfax, Va. in 1734 and drove his master's provision wagon over the Aleghanies in Braddock's campaign in 1775, remaining in service until the close. He is believed to be the last survivor of the expedition, either black or white.

42. At Brighton, Nova Scotia, Jan 6, George Sinnet, 120, sole survivor of the army of Gen. Wolfe. Took discharge from the 10th regiment 35 years ago. A native of Germany.

43. Isaac Vail was murdered at the residence of his late father Jacob Vail, in the town of Somers, on Sunday, the 14th inst. (White Plains Jour.).

44. Lieut. Thomas Mills died at Dunbarton, NH, on the 15th ult., aged 90 years. He was the first person in the town who enlisted to join Gen. Stark, at Bennington, in 1777, and among the first who went over to the enemy's breast works in that battle.

45. The brig Natahnis Fitch, of Pittston, Me., was run aground on Jan 26. The dead include: second officer Mr. George A. Gould, of Gardiner, Me.; Captain Andrew Fitch; George O. Bates of Springfield, Mass. and Thomas Pendergast, a native of Ireland.

4

46. Supposed loss of life in New York. On the 30th ult., after the Alle Pratte of Baltimore ran into the brig Cobden from Hamburgh. Probably drowned were Francis Neuhoff, A. Gunther, Carl Hesmann, Christopher Hesmann, Hemke Rudolf, Jo Seaman, Joseph Brown and Jack --- (Captain Cornish died not know his name).

February 17, 1849
47. Feb 9, drowned, James, son of James Flynn of this village, aged 6.

48. In the Virginia House of Delegates, on Friday last, Col. John W. Thompson, of Botetourt, died.

49. Notice to all debtors of the late Barnet Gay of the town of Saugerties to present demands to Joseph G. Gay. Saugerties, Jan 12th 1849.

50. William Wise, a blacksmith and Samuel Teerpenning, upwards of 60, a farmer, both residing near Cheney Ames' tavern at Amesville, town of Esopus, fought last week. Teerpenning stabbed Wise in the left groin severing the femoral artery. In five minutes Wise was a corpse.

51. A sail boat was upset in Niagara River on Friday night last. Four men were drowned. James Dixon, of Ohio, J. Mc Murray, T. Stevenson, and an old German, all from Canada. (Buffalo Express).

52. Mr. Zachariah Clapper, son of Jacob Clapper of this town, a brakeman, met his death in a railroad accident, leaving a family (Kinderhook Sentinel).

February 24, 1849
53. Monday last, in this town, Mary, wife of Anthony Jerver.

54. Feb 14, town of Kingston, Charles E. Joy, aged 36.

55. Feb 11, Wilbur, Catharine Ann, widow of James Philips, aged 89 years, 9 months.

56. Sunday last, Nottingham, NH, Mrs. Thomas was murdered. Her son, John, Jr., survives. (Nashua Telegraph).

57. The cholera still lingers at Houston. Among the victims are Col. John H. Walton, once Mayor of

5

Galveston. (Galveston Civilian, 24th ult.).

58. We find in the NY Tribune the following:
Isaac C. Betts, who was recently arrested in
Florence, Ohio, on a charge of having murdered his
brother John Betts, is said to have a wife and six
children in Ulster Co., in this State.

59. Colchester, in this county, Thursday last, Mr.
James Clapperton was killed by being hit with
logs. A blacksmith, age 45, he leaves a wife and
several children. (Del. Gazette).

60. Mr. Hall, one of the three persons who was
seriously injured by the fire in the 'Marble
Block', New Haven, has died. (Springfield
Republican).

March 3, 1849
61. Wednesday last, town of Florida, Reynolds
Snook, died after falling. (Montgomery Whig).

62. Friday night, Buffalo, Joseph Kelsey, tavern
keeper.

63. Thursday last, Hollis, NH, Hon. Timothy
Farrar, oldest surviving graduate of Harvard
University, born 11 July 1747, graduated 1767,
aged 101 years, 7 months and 10 days.

64. Peter Decker, 12, son of P. M. G. Decker of
this place, died on Tuesday evening. (Rondout
Courier).

65. A woman named Welch was killed on the railroad
tracks about a mile from Cartersville on Monday.
(Rochester Daily Advertiser).

66. The tavern house of Peter Valcott, near Fort
Wayne, was destroyed by fire a few days ago and a
son of Mr. V's perished.

67. Col. George H. Sands, of Middletown, Delaware
county, drowned himself in the East Branch of the
Delaware on Feb 24th. He was recently married.

68. The Macon (Geo.) Journal and Messenger of
Wednesday says: We regret to announce the death of
Hon. Edward D. Tracy, which took place at his
residence in this city yesterday morning.

March 10, 1849

69. Mrs. Walker was shot in the house of her husband in Lexington Avenue, NY. She died some hours later.

70. Notice: The settling of the accounts of John C. Burhans, deceased, dated March 10, 1849 by J. Foland.

March 17, 1849

71. Mar 12, Glasco, William Hendricks, aged 25.

72. The Calais Maine Journal relates the death by fire of two men between the ages of 17 and 18. One the son of Charles Ross of St. David, the other a son of Mr. Merrill Witcher, of St. Patrick.

73. A son of Mr. Charles Wakely, about 6, drowned in Canandaigua outlet in the rear of the premises of his grandfather, Mr. Thomas B. Dorsey of this town, on Monday last. (Canandaigua Repository).

74. Ithaca, Sunday, Hon. Timothy S. Williams, Senator from the 25th district of this state. (Albany Argus of Tuesday).

March 24, 1848

75. Tuesday last, in this town, Hannah, wife of John Teetsell, about 58.

76. Tuesday last, in this village, Margaret, wife of James Reed, aged 31.

77. Tuesday last, in this village, Mrs. Mc Kiefrey, wife of William Mc Kiefrey.

78. Wednesday last, west of Port Jervis, due to a premature explosion, Geo. Bruce was killed. He was employed as an overseer in the enlargement of the Delaware and Hudson Canal.

79. David C. Claypole, in his 96th year, died in Philadelphia a few days since. Reputed to be a lineal descendent of Oliver Cromwell.

80. Abby Pinnock, aged 17, a chambermaid in Boston, died from imprudent use of chloroform.

81. In Brownsville, Col. Louis P. Cook and wife died of cholera.

82. A melancholy accident occurred at Bayou Sara on last Sunday week. The wife and son of Mr. John Sulser were drowned. (N. O. Com. Bulletin of the 7th).

83. Warren, Bradford Co., Pa., Mar 11, 1839. <sic> The home of Charles Corben was burned. He and two sons, aged 7 and 13 were dead in the house.

84. In Pawtucket, two lads named Ramsbottom and Knight got into a fight. Knight died. (The Providence Transcript).

March 31, 1849
85. Tuesday last, Glasco, Mr. Nicholas Burhans, about 50.

86. Mar 13, Kingston, Luther H., infant son of Dumond Elmendorf.

87. Mar 21, Poughkeepsie, Gideon H. Osborn, about 47, a member of Dutchess Lodge # 59, IOOF.

88. A son of J. W. Hunter, of Corning, was burned to death on a raft lying in the Chemung River between Corning and Knoxville on Saturday evening last, in his 17th year. (Steuben Dem.).

89. New York, Sunday morning last, John L. Bookstaver, in his 30th year, a lawyer.

90. At Pittsburgh, Monday last in the explosion of Fife's vatting factory, Mr. J. Fife.

91. Died in the village of White Plains on the 11th of March, Rachel Jane, in her 8th year, on the Thursday evening following, Elisha B., in his 3rd year, and the succeeding Tuesday, Isiah, about 5, children of Mrs. Jane Maynard, the widow of Jeremiah Maynard, late of the town of Harrison. (Westchester Journal).

92. On Saturday, Lieutenant John E. Bispham, of the USN, died at his residence in Philadelphia.

93. Simon Shafer, of the city of New York, was killed on Wednesday week, while walking on the Erie railroad near Piermont.

94. On Monday of last week, in Emmet, Miss Elizabeth Welch, about 17, daughter of Michael Welch, met with a sledding accident. She died on

Thursday. (Washington (Maine) Chronicle).

April 7, 1849
95. Apr 3, in this village, of lingering
consumption, Miss Sarah Ann Post.

96. Mr. John H. Warren, Clerk to the Solicitor in
the Treasury Office, died on Monday night.

97. Woodson Smith, who fought valiantly during the
late war with Mexico, died of cholera on the 29th
inst., at his home in Memphis, Tenn.

98. The steamboat Defiance exploded below New
Orleans with three ships in tow. Mr. Mc Farland,
the first engineer, and three of the hands were
killed, and others injured.

99. Juan E. Trevana, a citizen of San Antonio, was
murdered by five Mexicans on the road between that
city and Laredo. Mr. Troller and his son are also
supposed to have been murdered, about 35 miles
south of San Antonio.

100. The fishing schooner Pearl, of Boothbay,
sunk. Dead include, Abraham Messenden, master;
George Mc Cobb, Ferdinand Mc Cobb, Thomas Hutchins
and Rufus Brewer, all of Boothbay, and all
unmarried men.

101. On Tuesday last, two sons of Leeds Dougherty
were fishing when a thunder shower came up. They
ran to a sycamore tree and were killed when
lightning struck it. (Cincinnati Com.).

April 14, 1849
102. Mar 28, Rondout, William Henry, child of John
and Elizabeth Snelling, aged 6 months.

103. Apr 3, Rondout, Caroline, child of John and
Elizabeth Snelling, aged 4 years.

104. Mar 31, Rosendale, Mr. Louis Auchmoody, in
his 29th year.

105. Mar 27, Rondout, Margaret, wife of James
Colvoy, aged 38.

106. Samuel Gould, colored, died on board the
steamboat Iolas, leaving a wife and child residing
in Greenbush.

107. Elijah Ball, who had been in the Rhode Island State prison for thirty years, for the murder of his wife, died on Wednesday.

108. George A. Durham, about 28, son of Jonathan Durham, of Belfast Me., committed suicide.

109. Tuesday evening last, between Kingston and Rondout. In the race of two stone wagons, Martin Ryan was killed; Peter Connor had an arm broken; James Connor's leg was dreadfully bruised and James Millan's face and head were shockingly lacerated. Ryan came from Dublin only a few days ago. (Rondout Courier).

110. John Allen killed himself at Norfolk Wednesday night, leaving a wife and children.

111. The Elizabethtown Register notes the damage from the tornado at Big Spring. A child of Samuel Knott, Mrs. Gorman and her child died, also at Hindingburg, Mr. Scot was killed. (Louisville Journal of the 28th ult.).

April 21, 1849
112. The body of Edmund Clark was found Thursday at the dock in Hudson. He leaves a wife and 4 children.

113. William Brown was killed on Friday last at Erie, by falling from the mast of the revenue cutter Erie.

114. Warren Miller was brutally murdered at Oak Shade, Culpepper co., Va. on Wednesday night.

115. About 2 o'clock on Saturday afternoon, Capt. Peter Vandewater, of the sloop Congress, when opposite Grand st., East River, fell overboard and was drowned.

116. Miss Newton, of Bennington, Vt., aged 20, left her bed on the night of the 9th inst., and wandered forth with only her nightclothes on. She was found drowned.

117. James Gillet, Esq., of Sodus, Wayne county, was bitten by a large hog just above the knee, and died in several weeks from the effects of the bite.

10

118. Lawrence Whalen was found dead in his cabin, at Vinegar Hill, Ill., on the 26th inst.

119. The steamer Lake of the Woods collapsed a flue on Grand River recently by which six persons were killed or scalded. Wm. Miller, first engineer died in 15 hours, Reuben Sun, deck hand, was blown overboard and drowned, Elijah Ward and Richard Kelley, deck hands, were badly scalded, George Mier and Angelrodt Gabter were slightly scalded.

120. Deaths from cholera at Brownsville, John Minsey, a carpenter, John D. Chamberlain, John H. Byrne and R. Breckenridge, the last not of cholera, all formerly of Galveston, also Capt. Young of the steamship Anson, a Mr. Kase and Geo. Grey, from Houston. Capt. George Bonner, of New Orleans, died of cholera at the Brazos on the 27th ult. (from Texas).

121. On the 11th at Wilmington, Mass., Mrs. H. P. Pierson and her twin daughters, aged 4, were killed.

April 28, 1849
122. Monday last, Glasco, Mr. Abraham Hendricks.

123. Saturday last, NYC, Mr. Eliphalet Miller, aged 21, burial in Saugerties.

124. Apr 17, Kingston, of consumption, Mr. Thomas Dewey, in his 36th year.

125. Apr 21, Kingston, John R. Schepmoes, aged 31.

126. Thomas A. Cooper, the distinguished tragedian, died at the residence of his son-in-law Robert Tyler, Esq., at Bristol, Pa., on Saturday last, in his 73rd year.

127. James Mc Cann, Jr. was convicted on the 4th inst., at Columbus (Miss.) of the murder of Andrew Toland, on the 14th day of April, 1845. Mc Cann will be hung.

128. Near Uniontown, Md., Mr. John Shriner was shot by his brother Mr. Wm. Shriner, a dental surgeon.

129. Mr. Frances Gottier De Liesseline, a
distinguished native of South Carolina, and a
soldier in the Revolution, died at St. Mary's,
Ga., on the 12th inst., aged 86. Burial in
Charleston.

130. Mr. Lawrance, of Cincinnati, has died at
Napoleon, Ark., from drinking cold water.

131. During a paroxysm of hydrophobia in York Pa.,
Conrad Zimmerman broke from his cords and cut his
throat.

132. Letters received in Marblehead tell that of
those who left the town for California, by the Rio
Grande route, Mr. Nathaniel B. Blaney, the leader,
has died of cholera, and Mr. Owen, of a NY
company, died about the same time, both nearing
Matamoras.

                    May 5, 1849
133. Tuesday last, in this town, Mrs. Catharine
Roosa, about 74.

134. Apr 30, Kingston, Nicholas Vanderlyn, aged 76
years, 3 months old.

135. Apr 25, Kingston, of puerperal fever,
Caroline, widow of John R. Schepmoes, aged 35.

136. Mar 21, Camp Ringgold, Starr County, Texas,
of Asiatic Cholera, Dr. Ravaud Kearny of NYC, in
his 27th year, nephew of the late General Kearny,
USA, and son of the late Rev. R. Kearny.

137. Recently in Troy, Catharine Morrissey, about
12, was burned to death at the poor house.

138. Wm. Thurston, aged 50, died in Utica while
racing horses.

139. Mathew Love, of Boston, poisoned himself to
death with rats bane on Monday morning.

140. Jas. Platt, 2nd, committed suicide at the
City Hotel in Oswego a few days since.

141. Elder Enos G. Dudley, convicted of the murder
of his wife in Grafton, NH, has been sentenced to
death, the execution to take place on the 23rd of
this month.

142. Mr. Jeremiah Anderson, a native of Eden, Me.
and first mate of the brig Franklin, was lost at
sea on the way from New Orleans to Boston.

143. In Baltimore on May 2, Mr. George Campbell
was killed by his brother-in-law John Price.

144. Sunday afternon near Five Points in NY, John
Monahan, a young Irishman, was murdered by William
Thompson.

145. Mr. Charles Austin, of Medford, NJ, died
suddenly in Philadelphia on Tuesday. His wife was
with him at the time.

146. Tuesday night on the North River, Thos.
O'Dougherty, a merchant of Madison, Hopkins Co.,
Ky., jumped overboard the steamboat Buffalo. His
mother resides in Cincinnati.

147. Coleman Hall shot his son, aged 15, at
Danville, NC. He mistook him for a turkey.

148. Mr. Houghtailing was decapitated by his 8
year old son on Apr 30. (NY Express).

May 12, 1849
149. Apr 7, in a letter from St. Petersburgh,
Russia, Major Whiseler has died of cholera.

150. C. Adams, of Stephentown, Rensselaer Co.,
hung himself a few days since because he had been
caught stealing turkeys. He was 22, had been
married 3 years, but never lived with his wife.

151. Mrs. Street, wife of W. P. Street and
daughter of Mr. Barnt W. Stryker of Gilboa,
committed suicide on the 22nd ult., by drowning
herself in Schoharie creek. She was in her 25th
year. (Prattsville Advocate).

152. Mr. Wm. J. Moore fell at 396 Water street,
New York and died on Monday last.

153. The Edgefield Advertiser (Ga.) states that
Mr. Richard Long was found dead in his bed.

154. On Monday last, Angeline Short, a girl
between 9 and 10 years of age, living with her
mother and her step-father Mr. Christian Waggoner,
in this village, was burned by her clothes
catching on fire. She died on Wednesday.

13

May 19, 1849

155. May 12, Kingston, Fanny Ellen Smith, widow of
Caesar Smith, colored, aged 48.

156. May 7, NYC, of consumption, Mary Ann, wife of
Phineas Pardee, formerly of New Salem, Esopus,
about 48.

157. Friday, Buffalo, James Weigenstein from
Watertown, about 18, died almost instantly as a
result of a kick from James Haggart, 20, of
Rochester.

158. The funeral of the late Right Rev. Morris
Brown, second Bishop of the African Methodist
Episcopal Church, took place at Philadelphia on
Monday afternoon. He was 80.

159. Dan Marble, the delineator of Yankee
character, died of cholera in Louisville. The
news was received in Boston by W. Warren, of the
Boston Museum, brother-in-law of Marble.

160. Mr. Vergnol, the Vice Consul of France to
Charleston, committed suicide on the 2d inst.

161. At Ceder Grove, NJ, Mrs. Nelson Van Syle and
a 4 year old infant died in a house fire.

162. The Louisville Courier of the 8th inst. notes
the following cholera deaths on the 7th. George
Roberts, merchant and Thomas Conn, recently
superintendent of the Kentucky River
improvements. The Courier of the 9th mentions the
deaths of Mr. Klinefelter, pilot of the Pittsburgh
packet Hibernia #2, and Mr. John Trueman, who died
of black tongue at Jeffersonville, yesterday.

May 26, 1849

The steamer Empire of Troy was struck by the
schooner Noah Brown near Newburgh on Thursday
March 18. Dead included several children, 3
unknown adults and: <#'s 163-168>

163. The wife of Gen. Noble of Essex Co., NY, aged
60.

164. Three brothers named Ladd, from Conn.,
emigrating west.

165. August Spinger, a German, aged 48.

166. John and Thos. Mc Cullough.

167. Janet Mc Garr, widow, Scotch woman.

168. William Arrig, an Englishman.

169. Died at San Antonio, Texas, on the 7th inst.,
Major General Worth, US Army, leaving a wife and
several children.

170. On the 15th inst., William Flint, about 50,
of Sydney, was instantly killed while moving a
building. He leaves a wife and 4 children.
(Delaware Gazette).

June 2, 1849
171. May 12, Rondout, Joseph Allcorn, aged 27.

172. May 16, near Ellenville, Mrs. Nancy, wife of
Joseph Townsend, aged 52.

173. Last night at Thomaston State Prison, Dr. V.
P. Coolidge committed suicide. He was confined
for the murder of Edward Mathews. (Boston
Traveller, May 19th).

174. Washington Goode, convicted of murder in
Boston, was executed in that city on Friday.

June 9, 1849
175. Tuesday last, in this village, of
consumption, David Burns, about 66.

176. Monday, Glasco, of cholera, Mr. Andrew Joy,
aged 70.

177. Tuesday, Glasco, Mr. James Du Bois, about
50.

178. Jun 1, town of Kingston, of cholera, Mr. Adam
Mautorstock, about 60.

June 16, 1849
179. Sunday last, in this village, David I. Pultz,
about 60.

180. Jun 5, Ellenville, of consumption, Mrs.
Margaret Miller, 25, wife of George Miller, and
mother of three small children.

181. May 31, Kingston, Robert Hasbrouck, aged 33.

182. Jun 10, Kingston, John, son of Abrm. T.
Vansteenburgh, aged 22 years and 5 months.

183. Joseph Washer, a resident of Norristown, was
crushed beneath the wheels of the cars on the
railroad near Manayunk on Saturday.

184. Mr. Thomas Greenfield, of Galena, Ohio, died
recently in consequence of taking some spirits of
turpentine, administered by his nurse, instead of
castor oil.

185. Ephraim Bowen committed suicide at Providence
on Saturday last, aged 70.

186. Col. Henry A. Livingston died at Poughkeepsie
on Saturday.

187. A man named Slack strayed in the Blast
Furnace Establishment at Stanhope and fell
asleep. He was suffocated.

188. A German laborer named Keysen, going from
Jersey City to Bergen Hill, was killed on the
cars.

189. Capt. J. B. Coffin, of the steamboat
Washington, died in Athens on the 8th inst., of
cholera.

190. Capt. Edward Deas, of the 4th US Artillery,
drowned from the steamer Yazoo near Rio Grande
City on the 7th inst.

191. J. H. Levy was killed in a violent storm at
Brazos on the steamer Herrera.

June 23, 1849

192. Jun 14, in this village, Jas. Dolan, about
35.

193. Jun 16, on board the steamboat R. L. Stevens,
James Featherson, aged 24, of this village.

194. Jun 18, in this village, Michael Mc Carthy.

195. Jun 20, in this village, James Wynn, about
45.

196. Jun 7, New Paltz, at the residence of her
father John Beaver, Esq., Mrs. Maria D. W., widow
of the late Solomon Bogardus, aged 26.

197. Jun 8, Rhinebeck Landing, at the home of his father John Radcliff, Esq., William Pitt Radcliff, aged 49.

198. May 21, Edgeworth town, Langford Co., Ireland, Maria Edgeworth, novelist, in her 83rd year. Daughter of Richard Lowell Edgeworth.

199. Martin Sharp, a German carman, died in Bloomfield, NJ.

200. Saturday afternoon, Scaghticoke, in the explosion of the powder mill of Loomis, Smith & Masters, John Gallagher, died and John Rouley was badly burned. (Troy Budget).

201. Inquest held Jun 9, at Rondout, on the body of William Bowers, 35, of Rosendale, who fell into the canal at High Falls two weeks previous.

202. Jun 17, at Louisville, Cassius M. Clay and Joseph Turner dueled. Turner is dead, Clay seriously wounded, but expected to recover.

203. New Orleans, on board the Crescent City, Mr. James Sinclair of Brooklyn, leaving a wife and daughter. He had 80 thousand dollars in gold dust on him at that time.

204. Mr. M. P. Denny, supposedly of New Orleans, died at Carthagena on board the Crescent City on the 6th inst.

205. James K. Polk, ex-President, died near Nashville, Tenn., on Friday Jun 15th, in his 54th year.

206. Hon. Tobias L. Hogeboom died of cholera at his residence in the town of Ghent, Columbia county on Wednesday week.

207. The Augusta, Ga. Chronicle of the 12th inst. gives the particulars of the murder of David Ross, of Putnam, Georgia, by his own son John Ross, on the 9th inst.

June 30, 1849
208. Jun 18, in this village, Michael Mc Carthy, aged 22 years, 6 months, born in Saugerties, child of John Mc Carthy of Saugerties.

209. Jun 28, in this village, Catharine Mc Carthy, aged 15 years, 18 days, born in NYC, child of John Mc Carthy of Saugerties. Truth Teller and Boston Pilot, please publish <#'s 208 & 209>

210. Jun 26, in this village, Mrs. Dillon.

211. Jun 21, Kingston, Maria Woodward, wife of Rodney N. Baldwin, Esq., aged 27 years, 9 months and 11 days.

212. Jun 22, Kingston, Inez, daughter of Francis C. and Ann Maria Voorhees, aged 5 months, 11 days.

213. Jun 19, Rondout, John, only son of John Dougherty, aged 14.

214. Yesterday, at Centre St. Hospital, Tom Flynn. (Sunday Times).

215. Inquest held Sunday on the body of John Rutlege, found floating in the creek at Rondout. (Kingston Journal).

216. Hudson, last Wednesday, Edward Cahoe, a native of Ireland, drowned. (Columbia Republican).

217. Hudson, on the railroad, Patrick Tynan, an Irishman, about 28, died. (Columbia Republican).

218. On Monday, Rev. Wm. B. Tappan, General Agent of the American Sunday school union, known as 'the American Montgomery' died of cholera in the Boston vicinity.

July 7, 1849
219. Jun 25, in this village, Mrs. Nelly Smith, relict of the late Lodowick Smith, about 67.

220. Jul 5, in this town, Peter B. Shub, about 38.

221. Friday, Malden, Mrs. Mary Rider, in her 90th year.

222. Saturday last, on board the steamer Norwich, of cholera, James D. Brink, of this village, 2nd engineer. (Rondout Courier).

223. Tuesday evening, Springfield, Ohio, James Richardson who belonged in Pennsylvania.

224. On the 20th inst., Connecticut River, by drowning, Mr. Henry Lay.

225. George Lee was drowned in the Outlet near the Exchange Mills on the 22nd inst., while bathing. An Englishman, he had been in this country about 2 months in the employ of Mr. Geo. Beuzeville as a harness maker. (Phelps, Ontario County Atlas).

226. The Lenox Star Extra of Cookville, Madison county, announces the sudden death on the 30th ult. by a kick from a horse of Dea. Alanson Wilcox, a prominent and estimable citizen.

227. Wednesday, in Lodi, Thatcher Swift, about 14, son of the Principal of the district school, was drowned. (Geneva Gazette).

228. Deaths from Woodbury, Gloucester county, NJ of cholera include: James Davis, two and one half hours after being taken; J. H. Herst, an Englishman, after eleven hours and David Mickle, taken on Thursday, died on Sunday.

229. Deacon Gardiner Smith of Hancock, Berkshire county, died of cholera. He had just returned from a visit to Albany. (Worcester Mass. Spy).

230. A German named Richards died of cholera in the Hudson county jail.

231. Miss Deforest and Mr. Addington were swept over the falls at Niagara.

232. A letter from Fort Kearney to Milwaukee, Wisc. announces the death of Hon. John J. Bevins of Southport, Wisconsin and formerly a member of the New York Legislature.

233. A colored man named Richd. Moore was drowned at Baltimore on last Friday afternoon.

234. The London papers announce the death of Hon. Sir Charles R. Vaughan who resided in this country in the capacity of Envoy Extraordinary.

235. The celebrated Madam Catalini died in Paris of cholera, aged 70. She... made an impression on the musical world never surpassed by that produced

by any other individual.

236. Robert Underhill was found dead on Friday
morning in a lot near the house occupied by Jacob
More, about a mile west of Malden.

237. Mr. Charles Crow, of Summit, Schoharie
county, was killed on Tuesday of last week by the
falling of a tree. His wife died on Wednesday,
leaving a babe and several small children.

July 14, 1849
238. Jul 9, in this village, John Ackerman.

239. Jul 4, Rochester, Ulster County, suddenly,
Peter M. Decker, aged 78 years, 10 months and 4
days.

240. Jul 1, Napanoch, Leger S. Hoyt, about 42.

241. On the 22nd ult., Goshen, NH, the widow
Elizabeth Griendell, 104 years, 3 months old.

242. John Wilder, Esq., an old and respectable
citizen of Wyoming County and for several years
Sheriff of Gennessee, was thrown from his wagon a
few days since and killed.

243. Col. Duncan, Inspector General of the US Army
died at New Orleans on Friday, the 6th inst.,
formerly from Orange county in this state.

244. Hannah A. Ferguson and Francis Sybil from NYC
and Mr. Jas. B. Strain were drowned in a mill pond
in South Worcester, Otsego Co. on the 30th ult.
(Delhi Gazette).

245. A sailor named John Smith, belonging to the
Canadian schooner Christina was found dead on the
night of the 4th. (Oswego Times).

246. Hermann Schwarz, German, was accidently
drowned on Tuesday afternoon, off Governor's
Island.

247. Three deaths from cholera in Saugerties
during the week. Barney Mc Graph, and William
Falchenmaker on Sunday, and Mr. Doyle.

248. Last Sunday, in this village, of cholera, Thaddeus D. Wilson.

249. Thursday, in this village, of cancer, Mrs. Lewis, wife of Peter I. Lewis.

250. Saturday last, in this town, of cholera, Mrs. Eliza More.

251. Jul 5, Kingston, Mary Adelia, wife of George W. Emigh, aged 20 years and 7 months.

252. Jul 13, Kingston, of consumption, Thomas Lucas, formerly of Newburgh, aged 62.

253. Jul 12, Rondout, Ida Frances, daughter of Joseph F. and Mary E. Davis, aged 9 months, 17 days.

254. Jul 13, Rondout, Lydia, wife of Edgar Hudler and daughter of Sol. I. Krom, of Rochester, aged 26.

255. Jul 13, NY, of the prevailing epidemic, Arthur Young Greeley, only son of Horace and Mary Y. C. Greely, aged 5 years, 3 months and 20 days.

256. Jul 12, New York, Mr. George Mc Neish, formerly of Kingston, aged 36.

257. Jul 9, Newburgh, at the residence of his son-in-law Daniel Deyo, Edward Hallock, in his 95th year.

258. On the 12th inst., Richmond, Chapman Johnson, in his 71st year.

259. Dr. Haddock, a native of New Hapmshire, and a relative of Daniel Webster, died of cholera in Buffalo on Thursday afternoon.

260. At High Falls on the 11th, a gunpowder disaster killed John Wheat, a contractor and badly burned Philip Travers. (Rondout Courier).

261. On Friday last in Kiskatom, Roswell Lawrance, son of Neely Lawrance, fell on a pitchfork and died. (Catskill Record and Democrat).

262. On Friday, Mary Hughes, an emigrant from Ireland fell senseless to the ground at Second

st., near avenue B in New York.

263. About midnight on the 9th inst., a storm commenced at Foster's Landing, Bracken Co., Ky. Drowned were Mrs. Smalley, her son and 2 daughters; Mrs. Paul and Miss Meachan.

264. Mrs. Dolly Madison, relict of James Madison, fourth President of the US, died at her residence in the city of Washington on the 12th inst., in her 84th year.

265. Jul 4, Stephen Shubert, a German, aged 24, died from a pistol shot.

266. Friday, Mrs. Dunne was stabbed by her husband, Mr. John Dunne, after he saw her with a clergyman in Gardiner Street, Hoboken.

267. Saturday, Ninth St., the foreman Wm. Higby was killed when the bed plates from the steamship Georgia fell.

268. Sunday at a bathhouse in Desbrosses st., Lewis Endle, a German, aged 37, died after jumping into the bath.

269. William Riston has been convicted of the murder of Edward Harris, at Baltimore, and is sentenced to be hung.

July 28, 1849

270. Sunday last, in this village, of cholera, Henry Farmer.

271. Jul 18, Kingston, of congestion of the lungs, Peter G. Sharp, aged 74.

272. Friday week, the execution of Matthew Wood, who murdered his wife, took place. Gov. Fish had twice respited the sentence.

273. A few days since, of cholera, Mr. Wyckoff, Treasurer of the Hudson River Rail Road Company.

274. A wonderful fatality recently marked the death of two brothers in Tisbemingo county, Mississippi. One, Rev. Elisha H. Rhodes, having died, the Rev. James Rhodes went to convey the intelligence to their mother, and on the way was struck by lightning and instantly killed.

275. Melancholy affair, Mrs. Royal, wife of John Royal of Monroe, Maine, on Tuesday week killed her only child, a daughter of five years, then hung herself.

276. On the 19th, Albany, Hon. Harmanus Bleeker, an esteemed citizen of Albany, aged 70.

277. Wednesday, last week, Mr. Elisha Smith, about 72, of Rockland, Sullivan county, shot James I. Nanery, 40, of the same town. Nanery leaves a wife and child.

278. Lund Washington, Jr. died at Washington on Thursday night, of cholera.

279. The son of Patrick Laughlin was drowned on Friday last at the Whaling Dock at Poughkeepsie.

280. The Louisville Courier of the 16th says that B. G. Cutter, a merchant, died of cholera.

281. Ebenezer Mack, a resident of Ithaca, Tompkins county, died there on Saturday the 14th inst. of consumption. Born in Kinderhook, Columbia County in 1791, aged 58.

282. Pierre Chonteau, the last surviving founder of St. Louis, died in that city, aged 91.

283. Mrs. Laurania Thrower died Mar 29th at her residence in Ogechee, at least 133. (Savannah Republican).

284. The Rev. Alexander Vancourt, pastor of the Third Presbyterian Church in St. Louis, died of cholera on the 23d. A member of the Odd Fellows.

285. S. Mansfield Bay, Esq., formerly of Hudson, now of St. Louis, died in that city of cholera.

286. Saturday, Wm. H. Bradley, died of cholera, as did his eldest daughter, aged 11, on Sunday. (Poughkeepsie Telegraph).

287. On the 15th, Richmond, a man named Cook was shot by a man named Latten.

August 4, 1849
288. Sunday last, in this village, Mrs. F. Kearnon, about 55.

23

289. Jul 25, Kingston, of diarrhea, Richard
Francis, son of Richard Luther, aged 4 years, 5
months.

290. Jul 30, Kingston, of cholera, Almina Luther,
wife of Richard Luther, aged 47.

291. Aug 1, Kingston, Richard Luther, about 55.

292. Jul 22, High Falls, Catharine, wife of Jacob
I. Signer, about 45.

293. On the 29th ult., Rondout, of the prevailing
epidemic, Marie, wife of John P. Davis, aged 58.

294. Monday, two miles from Newburyport, Mass., J.
N. Jacques was killed in a rail road accident. He
was about 50.

295. On the 20th, the body of Michael Welch, a
cook on the schooner Eudore, of Buffalo, was found
floating in the river near Oswego.

296. The Washington papers announce the death of
Charles Porter, the body servant of the President,
of apoplexy.

297. Among the victims of cholera at Buffalo, the
wife of Dr. Foote of the Commercial Advertiser.
(Argus).

298. Nathan Huffman shot Wm. Mayo at Jefferson
City, Mo., on the 10th inst., killing him on the
spot. Huffman escaped.

299. Judge Thomas Henry, one of the pioneers of
Beaver, Pa., died at Beaver on the 20th, aged 68.

300. Gen. John I. Morgan died Sunday at the
residence of his son-in-law, Gen. John A. Dix, at
Port Chester, Westchester County, in his 81st
year.

301. On Thursday last, Mr. Cornelius Lansing of
Watervliet, was found dead in his barn, gored by a
bull.

302. Monday, J. N. Jacques, of Newburyport, Mass.,
committed suicide on the railroad.

August 11, 1849

303. On the 31st ult., Charleston, SC, Lieut. F. A. Deas, USN.

304. Sunday last, in this village, of cholera, Ellen, daughter of Patrick Lynch, about 18.

305. Sunday last, in this village, of cholera, Rosa Riley, wife of Edward Riley, about 50.

306. Thursday, in this village, of cholera, John Brown.

307. Sunday last, in this village, of cholera, James Doyle.

308. Wednesday, in this village, of cholera, Mr. Loyd.

309. Wednesday, in this village, John, son of Thomas Edwards, about 4.

310. Aug 7, Kingston, Mary Elizabeth, only daughter of Jacob P. and A. M. Osterhoudt, aged 2 years, 6 months and 16 days.

311. Aug 5, Kingston, Harriet Emeline, daughter of William Curran, aged 3.

312. Aug 1, Goshen, Albert S. Benton, Clerk of Orange County.

313. Jul 8, Rondout, John Jenkins, son of Rev. B. T. and M. E. Phillips, aged 11 months, 19 days.

314. John Vashaw, overseer on the railroad, died after a quarrel. (Poughkeepsie Journal).

315. Two lads named Nelson Dole and Alexander Gowe were drowned at the acqueduct near Schenectady, a few days since.

316. We learn that Capt. M. H. Truesdell, long known as a popular steamboat commander, died on the 29th ult. at Coxsackie, after a few hours illness.

317. The Mayor of Frederick, Md., M. E. Bargis, Esq. died on Monday at his residence.

318. On Friday last, the house of Mr. Moulton in West Newbery took fire. Captain Thomas Chase at

25

once went to render assistance but, upon arriving, fell dead in a fit.

319. In St. Louis, five practising physicians have died of cholera: Dr. Hardage Lane, Pollock, Farrer, Drake and Barbour.

320. At the canal near the Hamilton Counting Room, Lydia Jane Tracey, about 18, a milliner, drowned. (Lowell Courier, 4th).

August 18, 1849

321. Monday last, in this village, Adelaide Elvireta Richmond, daughter of Abner H. and Electa Richmond, aged 4 years, 6 months and 2 days.

322. Aug 11, in this village, Emma, only daughter of John and Caroline C. Simmons, aged 3 years, 6 months and 6 days.

323. Aug 10, in this village, Lydiaette, youngest daughter of Richard Rustin, about 1 year and 10 months old.

324. Monday last, in this village, of cholera, John Mc Adams, about 45.

325. Wednesday last, in this village, of cholera, Catharine Mc Adams, about 40.

326. Monday last, in this village, of consumption, William Patterson, about 50.

327. Aug 10, in this town, of cholera, Benjamin Swart, about 50.

328. Friday, in this town, of cholera, Patrick Mooney.

329. Aug 15, Kingston, of cholera, Francis Rhineheart, about 50.

330. Aug 9, Kingston, Isaac B., son of Isaac B. Krum, aged one 1 year and 9 months.

331. Aug 14, Kingston, of cholera, Mrs. Susannah Wiltsie, widow of John Wiltsie, aged 84.

332. Aug 2, Flatbush, Hannah Olivit, wife of Jonathan S. Olivet.

333. Aug 7, Flatbush, Maria, wife of Cornelius Legg, in her 83rd year.

334. Jul 31, Flatbush, John Aaron, son of Elizabeth M. and George W. H. Sisum, in his 4th year.

335. Monday last, Poughkeepsie, Robert Wilkinson, Esq., in his 63rd year.

336. Jul 31, Port Benjamin, town of Wawarsing, Frances Maria, youngest daughter of Lewis and Margaret Lawrence, aged 1 year, 4 months.

337. Jul 6, New York, of pleurisy, Maria Kellogg, wife of Epenetus Kellogg, formerly of this county.

338. Mr. John Wise murdered Thos. Hart at Palmyra, Mo., on the 2nd inst.

339. Sunday last, Astoria, LI, Hon. Albert Gallitin, born in Geneva, Switzerland, Jan 29, 1761.

340. Last week in Durham, NH, John O. Odell, aged 17.

341. Joseph Lewis, about 25, a native of Newburyport, died on Saturday afternoon. (Boston Transcript).

342. Yesterday afternoon, Mount Auburn, M. Hannibal H. Hildreth, committed suicide. His wife died last Sunday.

343. On the 13th inst., Poughkeepsie, of typhus fever, Robert Wilkinson, Esq., in his 63rd year.

344. Isaac Dimond, about 25, met with an accident while engaged at his work in the paper mill in this village, on Monday last, which resulted in his death.

August 25, 1849
345. Aug 12, Kingston, of cholera, Mary, daughter of Thos. Radcliff, recently of Poughkeepsie, aged 10 years.

346. Aug 10, Rondout, the widow of Abm. Van Schaick.

347. Aug 15, Rondout, of cholera, Abraham, son of the late Abm. Van Schaick, about 20.

348. Friday last, Poughkeepsie, Sarah Jane, wife of James Trivett, and daughter of Joseph I. Jackson of Fishkill, aged 35.

349. Aug 18, Poughkeepsie, of convulsions, Elizabeth, twin sister of Anna, and daughter of W. P. and Mary R. Gibbons, aged 8 months and 2 days.

350. William Leete Stone died Aug 15, 1844, aged 52 and Obed M. Coleman died April 5th 1845, aged 28, both buried at Saratoga Springs, from a letter to the editor.

351. On the 14th, Marbletown, of cholera, Mr. George Bastian. His wife died on the 19th. (Kingston Journal).

September 1, 1849
352. Aug 28, in this village, at the home of John Simmons, Jr., Miss Emma Campbell, about 28, late of Mass., and sister of Caroline C. Simmons, wife of John.

353. Aug 30, in this village, at the home of John Simmons, Jr., Miss Lucy Ann Campbell, about 25, late of Mass., and sister of Caroline C. Simmons, wife of John.

354. Thursday, in this village, Abraham Coon, about 50.

355. Aug 25, Kingston, Emilie Shaffer, daughter of Charles W. and Caroline Shaffer, aged 3 years, 3 months and 11 days.

356. Aug 25, Kingston, Riley Rich, aged 42.

357. Aug 23, town of Kingston, Christopher Van Gaasbeek, Jr., aged 53.

358. Aug 24, Kingston, Margaret C. Howe, wife of James Howe, aged 38.

359. Aug 21, Rondout, of cholera, James Houghtaling, master of the scow sloop Don Juan, aged 30.

360. Aug 21, Rondout, of cholera, Erasmus Rhodes, of Milton, a hand on the Don Juan, about 20.

361. Joseph Bradshaw, recently from New York, aged 19, died Monday, at Barnum's Museum Building, Philadelphia.

362. Daniel M. Cooley died at his home in Schuyler, Herkimer county. (Utica Observer).

363. Alonso Warden, aged 18, drowned Friday last, in the Piscataguis River.

September 8, 1849
364. Thursday, in this village, of consumption, Henry Matthews.

365. Saturday, Quarryville, of cholera, Lyman Overbagh, about 32.

366. Saturday, Quarryville, of cholera, Catharine, wife of John Waters.

367. Sep 4, Kingston, Thomas Dyer, aged 50.

368. Sep 4, Kingston, John Van Steenbergh, about 50.

369. Sep 2, Kingston, Augustus Freer, son of George Perrine, aged 2.

370. Sep 1, Rondout, of consumption, Rev. Myles Maxwell, Pastor of the Catholic Congregation of that place.

371. The Rev. Elijah Crawford of the ME Church died in New York on the 30th of August, aged 35.

372. George Martin drowned while bathing in the Chemung River, at Binghampton, on the 29th. Lewis Seymour drowned while trying to save him, leaving a wife and 6 children.

373. On the 27th ult., Thomas Hammond, aged 3 and 1/2, of Weathersfield, Wyoming county was burned. He died 36 hours later.

374. Saturday last, Garrit E. Russell, Esq., near 60, editor of the Argus of Western America.

375. On Wednesday last five persons were drowned in the Susquehanna River about one mile from Safe Harbor, while attempting to cross in a skiff. Their names are Mrs. Manning, Miss Hughes, 19; David Rowland, Mr. Peters and a son of Peters,

about 14.

376. Rev. Dr. Ernst, President of the Lutheran
Synod, died at Lebanon, Pa. on Saturday last of
Cholera Morebus.

377. The New York Day Book says: A letter has been
received here dated San Francisco, Upper
California announcing the death of George L.
Humphrey, formerly of Albany, also stating that
his brother William was in good health. They
belonged to Company H, New York Volunteers.

378. The noted Maria Monk died in the Alms House
on Blackwell's Island on Tuesday last says the New
York Merchant's Ledger.

379. Capt. A. Tyson, late commander of a US snag
boat on the Mississippi river, was shot in the leg
by one of his negroes, while asleep in bed, and he
bled to death. (Louisville Journal).

380. Mr. Conkin, a merchant of Peoria, Ill., died
of cholera.

381. Mr. Anderson of Vache Crasse, Arkansas was
murdered by his slave on the 4th ult.

382. Sep 15, at Suffrans & Sons brick manufactory,
in Memphis, a man named Hill accidently shot a man
named White.

September 15, 1849
383. Sep 12, in this village, William Stephens,
son of Rev. C. Van Santvoord, aged 7 months, 20
days.

384. Saturday last, Malden, Stephen Calkin, aged
29.

385. Aug 28, Flatbush, Mr. Timothy Lawrence, aged
70 years, 2 months, and 28 days.

386. The Hon. A. Newman, member of Congress elect
from Virginia, died at Pittsburg on Saturday.

387. Hon. Edward J. Black, of Scriven county,
formerly a representative in Congress from Ga.,
died on Sep 1. (Ga. Constitutionalist).

388. Western papers mention the death of Hon. Amos
Lane, at his residence near Aurora, Ind.

389. The brig Stambach capsized on the 29th ult. about 10 miles northwest of Fairport, 3 died, Horace Bush, Irwin Joiner and Horace Crandall, all belonging to Conn. (Painsville (O.) Telegraph).

390. W. W. B. Luidley, the extensive sewing silk manufacturer, died of cholera at South Woburn, Mass. last Thursday.

391. We learn from the Troy Budget of Friday that Ellen Maria Haley, about 12, was injured by the cars on the bridge and died soon after.

392. A rail-road accident occurred at Syracuse on Tuesday afternoon, by which Mr. F. A. Fargo of Albany was killed.

393. We regret to learn, says the Albany Argus, the sudden death of Mr. John Slack, of Guilderland.

394. As the stevedores were unloading the ship Washington at New York on Saturday last, they found, packed away among the boxes in the lower hold, the body of Charles Page, 21, a Prussian. He had disappeared on Aug 15.

395. The Paulding (Miss.) Clarion learns that on the evening of the 21st, on the Mobile road, Mr. Jesse Cole, well known citizen, was shot upon his horse, and almost instantly killed by a man named Clark.

396. On Saturday last, says the Rondout Courier, Mr. Turner, from Phillipsport, up the canal, and a boy named Frost, from Middleport, in this county, were involved in an accident. Frost was killed.

397. On the 2d inst., New York, P. Bryon Barker, formerly of Hudson, died. (Hudson Republican).

398. Saturday, Pittsford, railroad conductor John Sholtus was killed in an accident. (Rochester Democrat).

399. At Ida Hill, John Moseley was killed while fixing machinery.

September 22, 1849

400. Sep 13, Wilbur, Mary Elizabeth, daughter of Thomas and Mary A. Booth, of this place, aged 14 months.

401. Saturday last, in this village, Mrs. Elizabeth York, in her 70th year.

402. A young man named Philip Petona died yesterday morning at one of our cotton factories. He was bitten by a rat on the chin 2 weeks ago. His face swelled to a frightful extent, all known remedies were applied, but they failed, and he died in extreme pain. (Wheeling Age).

403. The N. York papers announce the death of Rev. Thomas Burch, well known in the Methodist Church.

404. John Houghtailing, of Esopus, (says the Rondout Courier) aged about 20 years, a fireman on the steamer Norwich, was accidently killed on the passage up last Tuesday.

405. The New Haven Register reports the murder of Mrs. Olive Foote and Emily Cooper, a young girl in the house, by H. Leander Foote.

406. An inquest was held at Manheim on the 5th inst. on the drowned corpse of Mrs. Catherine, wife of Archibald Van Allen, about 45 and her son 17 months old. (Herkimer Democrat).

407. The Hudson Republican of the 10th says, "The body of Mr. Charles Smith, of that city, was found drowned in 'Livingston's Creek' on Tuesday last.."

408. Mr. Israel Post, well known as a book and magazine publisher of New York, died of cholera at Panama on the 6th.

409. Capt. R. H. Floyd, of Brooklyn, last of the US Army, died at Panama on the 13th of cholera.

410. Jennette, daughter of Mr. Henry Hall, of Litchfield, Conn. was so seriously injured by being kicked by a horse on Wednesday last, that she died in a few hours.

411. Inquest held at Malden on the body of Robert Locke, of West Troy, employed as a hand on board the vessel James North, death resulted from violence.

412. Sep 13, East Hartford, Conn., a powder mill
kept by Hammer and Forbes blew up, killing John
O'Brien, aged 27.

September 29, 1849
413. Sep 22, Kingston, Sarah E., daughter of
Andrew E. and Elsey Schepmoes, aged 5 months, 3
days.

414. Sep 19, Kingston, Louriett, daughter of
William Williams, aged 1 year, 7 months.

415. Near Palatine Grove, Ill., about the 3rd
inst., a young girl named Salina Montgomery, 15,
who was supposed to have some knowledge of the
movements of a band of horse thieves, was murdered
by being thrown into the creek. A man named
Samuel Perkins, who, it is supposed, was hired to
secrete the body, when an effort was made to
arrest him, blew his brains out with his musket.

416. Friday, at the opening of the Concord and
Clarmont Railroad to Warner, Mr. Harvey Gould, of
Warner, was thrown under a car and killed.

417. Friday, a blast on the Hudson River Railroad
killed Michael Rafferty, and one other man, and
injured 15 others.

October 6, 1849
418. Oct 4, Coxsackie, Robert Brown, Jr., about
18.

419. Thursday of last week, N. York, fire claimed
the lives of James Kegan and a woman named Gaylard
who had been married for 4-5 weeks.

420. The Cleveland Plaindealer says that the Schr.
Lasalle capsized in a gale off Racine. Dead
include Capt. A. N. Scott, mate Henry Griffin,
Charles Stewart and 5 unknowns.

421. On Sunday, John Beekman fell from the
gangplank of the steamer Norwich and died. He was
about 26, a native of Kingston. (Rondout
Courier).

422. Judge Thomas Hertell, of NY city, died on
Monday morning, aged 78.

423. Frederick Stahl, a native of Germany, and his
daughter, died at Berks county alms house.

(Reading Press).

424. Chas. I. Ruggles, Attorney and Counselor at Law, died at Poughkeepsie on the 25th ult.

425. Robert H. Murphy, of Westerlo, a Deputy Sheriff of Albany county, died while in the performance of his duty as a public officer.

426. Sep 27, Charles, son of John Cooley, residing near Wilbur, was drowned from the dock near his home, in the Rondout Creek. (Kingston Journal).

October 13, 1849
427. Oct 9, in this village, Elizabeth, wife of Dr. William C. Dewitt.

428. Sep 29, Shawangunk, at the residence of her son-in-law Sylvenus M. Bruyn, Elizabeth, relict of James Hasbrouck, in her 83rd year.

429. Edgar A. Poe, well known author, died at Baltimore on Sunday last.

430. Elinor Mc Crackan, recently from Ireland, drowned herself in Lower St. Clair township, Pa. on Monday.

431. Jonathan Burns killed his wife at Claysville (Ky.) on the 12th ult.

432. Mr. Robert Evans, residing in Parish street, Philadelphia, was burned to death on Saturday evening by the explosion of a camphine lamp.

October 20, 1849
433. Oct 11, Rondout, Catherine, daughter of Wm. Throp, and wife of E. S. Stout, aged 18 years, 10 months.

434. Oct 6, High Falls, Isaac D. W. Robinson, aged 70.

435. The Rev. James Nichols of Caroline Co. (Md.) recently shot and killed Miss Juliet Nichols.

436. Mr. Elisha Denison, of Portersville, aged 50, hung himself, leaving children.

437. W. West, of Peru, Clinton county, was accidently shot on Friday week, while gunning in the woods.

October 27, 1849

438. Oct 12, in this village, Mrs. Hannah France, relict of Philip France, about 73.

439. Oct 22, in this town, of consumption, Wm. F. Hawley.

440. Christopher Joselyn was beaten to death on Sunday night in Albany.

441. Alonzo Day, of Glen's Falls, was killed on Monday at Schenectady, by being run over by the cars.

442. Ira King was killed on Saturday last, on board the steamer Westpoint.

443. Bridget Howel, a servant in Mr. Johnson's establishment on Fulton street, NY, died of burns on Saturday.

November 3, 1849

444. Oct 28, in this town, of consumption, John Plough, about 63.

445. Mr. James Simson, of Thompsonville, died about a week ago. (New Haven Register).

446. Benjamin F. Baker, aged 46, of Onondaga Hollow, committed suicide.

447. Dr. Peter Wendell, Chancellor of the University, died at his residence in Albany on Monday the 29th, an Albany native, aged 64.

448. The Dansville Chronicle announces the death of Major Moses M. Van Campen, in his 94th year at Angelica.

449. A Hawkinsville correspondent of the Augusta Constitutionalist tells of a murder committed by two men on the person of speculator John G. Ponder, who was on his way to Florida with a drove of negroes. The murderers have not been discovered.

450. Daniel Bozry, a sawyer in the employment of John Post, Esq., lumber merchant at Aquacknock, NJ, came to his death on Monday afternoon.

451. While on board the steamer Hudson, from NY to Hudson, Robert Stott was stabbed by Joseph

Flouton. Stott leaves a wife and child.

452. Ferdinand Rowe killed a man named James at
Lime. (Watertown Journal).

453. Mrs. Abbot was strangled by two negros in
Arkansas. (Eldorado Union).

454. The Clearspring, Md. Sentinel, of Saturday,
states that a man named Cox was buried by an
avalanche.

November 10, 1849
455. On the 27th ult., Mrs. Baker, wife of Zenus
W. Baker of Sandusky City, Ohio, died, aged 51.

456. Thursday evening, 18th inst., Southport, in a
house fire at the residence of John Townsend,
Martin Townsend, 14 and James H. Hardy, nearly 8,
died. (Chemg. Dem.).

457. The ship Roland was wrecked about one half
mile from shore at Mazatlan on the 10th of August.
About 25 men were drowned including Major
Cornelius Taylor, formerly of Matamoras county.

458. Charles Smith and wife, an aged couple, were
murdered near New Haven.

459. Lieut. Col. Dickinson, of the Palmetto
Regiment, died recently.

460. On Sunday, James Corbitt suffered an accident
and died on Tuesday, leaving a wife and family of
children. (Danbury Times).

November 17, 1849
461. Oct 23, in this village, Anna Myre Post,
youngest daughter of Samuel M. and Nelly Post,
aged 2 years and 5 days.

462. Maj. Chauncey B. Gidney, a citizen of this
town, about 50, and uncle to Charles Gidney, died
recently. (Newburgh Excelsior).

November 24, 1849
463. Michael Bless (or Blessene) a laborer on
section 46 of the Hudson River Railroad, was
killed on Monday of last week.

464. Nov 3rd, in Poughkeepsie, Jane Eliza, only
daughter of Wm. and Eliza Hill, aged 6 months and

25 days.

465. Mr. Halloway Fullerton, aged 28, son of Judge Fullerton of Minisink and brother of Wm. Fullerton of Newburgh, died near Salisbury, Orange county, while attempting to jump from one car to another, while in motion, on the Chester Railroad.

466. The Westminister, Md. Carroltonian states that a colored man named Charles Robertson, owned by M. G. Cockey, Esq., of Finksburgh, Carroll county, died on Friday last, aged 103 years and 7 months, leaving a daughter aged 81.

467. A man named Henry Rowe drowned in the creek at Catskill on the 13th inst.

468. The Montreal Courier tells of an accident on the steamboat Comet, two firemen died, Matthew Nolan and Michael Ring.

469. Friday, Mr. William R. Mc Cullough, agent of the NY and Saugerties White Lead Company, drowned.

December 1, 1849
470. Nov 23, Kingston, Delia, wife of Robert C. Holdrige, aged 27 years and 9 months.

471. Nov 16, Plattekill, Benjamin Roberts, in his 68th year.

472. C. A. Snyder, carpenter, of Philadelphia, was shot dead there on Friday evening last.

473. An inquest was held on the body of Edward Sloughter, colored, aged 13, of Esopus, accidently drowned at Creek Locks on the 20th. (Rondout Courier).

474. John Mc Clusky, about 30, an Irishman, died on Sunday night. (Rondout Courier).

December 8, 1849
475. Tuesday last, Flatbush, John H. Plough, about 32.

476. Dec 1, Flatbush, Rachael Lawrence, wife of David Griffin, aged 28.

477. Nov 24, Troy, NY, Susanna, wife of James Beckley of this village, aged 57.

478. Four men were killed on the Fitchburg road, Timothy O'Connor, David Barre, Martin Mc Can and James Fitzgibbon, all 25-30. (Boston Traveller of Saturday).

479. On Tuesday afternoon Mr. James Dewitt, of this town, hung himself, 25-26 years of age, leaving a wife and three small children, the youngest but 4 days old.

480. Derrick Plass of Greenport, Columbia county, and one of the Orbit's company, died at the California mines in August last, in the 20th year of his age.

December 15, 1849
481. Friday, Miss Mary Hughes, 17, daughter of Mr. Lloyd Hughes of Ritchietown, committed suicide by drowning.

482. Philo Redmond was murdered on the Schenectady turnpike on Thanksgiving night.

483. The Rev. Peter Rogers, one of Washington's Life Guards, died in Illinois, aged 96, the last of that faithful band.

484. Tuesday, near Frederick, Md., Mr. George W. Cook was thrown from his horse and died.

485. Brevet Captain Warner died on Sep 27th while engaged in ascertaining the feasibility of a rail-road to Oregon through the head sources of the Sacramento. (Calif. news).

486. Peter Black and John Black were hung for mutiny and desertion on Oct 23 in San Francisco. Three other sentences were commuted to 3 years, Jonathan Biddy, Wm. Hale and Henry Cummerford.

487. A violent tornado in Adams county, Miss., killed Mr. Mc Culloch.

December 22, 1849
488. Aaron Day, veteran of the Revolution, died at Blodgett's Mills, Cortland county, on the 24th ult., aged 81.

489. Mrs. Walbridge, 42, mother of nine children, accidently fell in Bushnell's basin near Rochester, and drowned. They were travelling west on the canal.

490. Charles Mullaly, a laborer on the Erie Railroad was run over by the cars, near Port Jervis, on the 13th and so much injured as to cause his death.

491. Adam Post, while walking on the railroad track, between Dillersville and Little Conotoga Bridge, was killed by the train.

492. Orrin T. Palmer, one of the employers of the Hudson River Railroad, was instantly killed at Fishkill on Tuesday by a train.

December 29, 1849
493. Tuesday morning, in this village, Mrs. Charlotte D., wife of Solomon A. Smith, aged 32.

494. Dec 25, in this village, Mrs. Elizabeth Elting, 52 years old.

495. Sunday last, in this town, Adam Brink, about 89, a soldier of the Revolution.

496. Hon. Eben B. Morehouse, one of the Justices of the Supreme Court of the 6th Judicial District, died in Cooperstown on the 16th inst.

January 5, 1850
497. Saturday, during the sinking of the schooner Ellen Sedgwick, 7 hands including Capt. Besston, of Brooklyn, died.

498. On the 30th ult., East Worcester, Otsego county, George Rice, aged 45.

499. On the 20th ult., Kempton, Washington county, William Miller, also known as Father Miller and Miller, the prophet, about 68, founder of the 'Milerites', died.

January 12, 1850
500. On the 16th ult., Pocahantas county, Va., Miss Melinda Wanless, 16, drowned while endeavoring to ford a stream on horseback.

501. The St. Louis Republican announces the death, in that city, of Wm. M. Campbell, an eminent lawyer and Robert Ranken, an opulent merchant.

January 19, 1850
502. Jan 4, Kingston, Mr. Isaac Post, in his 38th year.

503. San Antonio river, Texas, James G. Faulk was killed, J. B. Patterson badly wounded, while making an attack on the house of Mr. Patterson.

504. Last Tuesday, St. Lawrenceville county, NY, John Keeler smothered while sitting up to watch a fire made for the purpose of drying the plaster in a new home.

505. Last Tuesday, Mr. John Alleman, a shoemaker of Philadelphia, was burned by upsetting a camphene lamp and died.

506. Mary Smaftz drowned in the Kentucky river, near Frankfurt.

507. Mrs. Robinson, of Bowling Green Ky., fell from the rail of a steam boat last week, while talking, and was drowned.

508. The St. Lawrence Mercury notices the death of Mr. Thomas Meecham of Hopkinton, in that county, who resided several years in township No. 10, Franklin county, and was a celebrated hunter. He kept an exact account of all game killed by him: wolves 214, panthers 77, bears 219, deers 2550.

509. Mr. Verbeyst, most celebrated book collector in the world, recently died at Brussels at an advanced age.

510. Mr. John Bell, formerly treasurer of New Orleans, has died in California.

511. Mrs. Gore was crossing Tremont st., Boston, on the 2d inst. She either slipped or was thrown down by a team of three horses, and killed. A native of New Gloucester, Maine and about 72.

512. The Wheeling Gazette notes that James Garl died by falling off a precipice on Sunday evening.

513. Died at Osterville, Mass., on Monday Dec 21st, Benj. Hallett, in his 90th year. He served in the Revolution both by land and sea. Father of Hon. B. F. Hallett, of Boston.

514. The Vicksburgh Whig states that a man named Myrick was murdered in Hindes county, by his son, on the 25th ult.

515. A young son of Mr. Isaac Bell of St. Louis, was drowned while ice skating.

January 26, 1850
516. Jan 21, Jordanville, Shawangunk, Mary, infant daughter of Selah T. and Mariah Jordan.

517. Jan 11, Woodstock, of typhus fever, Mary Pecore, wife of Elias Hasbrouck, about 40.

518. Captain Connor of the US Revenue Service died on the 11th inst. at Erie, about 50 and weighing 450 pounds.

519. John Mc Cune, who met with an accident on the Hudson River Railroad, a short time ago, and for which his leg was amputated last week in the Hospital, NY, died there on Wednesday.

520. Maj. Henry L. Prentiss, a well known citizen of Quincey, Ill., was brutally murdered in that city on Christmas eve, by two young men named Wert and Armor.

521. Captain Alexander G. Gorden, of the US brig Porpoise, died at Port Grand, Island of St. Vincent on the 11th of October last.

522. Mr. John Richards, the superintendent of the Franklin paper mill in Richmond, Va., was killed on Wednesday.

523. Isaac Musselman and Toner, lunatics, were chained to the floor of the Gettysburgh, Pa. prison when it burnt last week, and both perished in the flames.

524. A daughter of Hiram Cass, of Brandon, Vt., came to her death a few days ago by tying a strap round her own neck and around the neck of a pet calf which ran away and choked the child.

525. Nancy Thompson, colored, aged 64, of West Centre street, Boston, died Sunday last of burns.

526. Terace Coulin, 17, died in Pawtucket on the 15th inst. (Providence Journal).

527. Elias Knight, of Kentucky, committed suicide on the 7th inst.

528. On Jan 7th, Charles Augustus Heintzman, a
German, aged 28, of South Rondout, drowned.
(Rondout Courier).

529. We learn from the Rondout Courier of last
week that William Culley, for many years an editor
in this county, died at Richmond, Va., in August
last. From the Ulster Republican, of this week,
we learn that his brother John Culley, a veteran
printer, died a few months previous.

530. The Natchitoches papers record the decease of
Judge James Taylor.

531. The recent butchery of Judge Van Winkle and
his wife were the first murders ever committed in
Passaic county.

February 2, 1850
532. Monday, Boston, Mr. Cosmo Lund, died as a
result of a railroad accident.

533. On Monday morning a man named Patrick
Callaghan died in the City Hospital, NY from
erysipelas, brought on by wearing a tight boot.

534. Saturday last, Honesdale, Pa., the daughter
of Judge Woodward of Wilksbarre, and two of her
friends, died while sliding on ice which gave.

535. David Hartshorn, in his 60th year, who had
resided in that village, committed suicide on
Monday last. (Poughkeepsie Telegraph).

536. An inquest was held on the body of Nathan
Leonard, 60, found frozen at Pine Kill,
Wurtsborough. He had been a school teacher, and a
minister and elder in the Baptist Church at
Westmoreland, NH.

537. The Toronto Globe reports the trial of Jacob
Nell for the murder of his wife Maria, in
November. He was found guilty and sentenced to be
hanged Feb 7.

February 9, 1850
538. Pena y Pena, for a time President of the
Mexican Republic, died recently in the city of
Mexico.

539. An old man by the name of Thomas Bennett, who
had been, for a long period, doorman at the

Fourteenth Ward Station House, died from the effects of poison.

540. The dead body of Mr. Roberts, about 55, of Milford, was found near the track of the New York Railroad between Milford and Orange.

541. A very extraordinary death occurred in New York. Mrs. Amelia Waugh was found by her husband, upon going to dinner, sitting in her chair with her face resting in a pan of dried peas on the table. Peas were found in her mouth, nose and under her eyelids, and it was found that she died of congestion of the lungs from suffocation.

542. Hiram Vorus, of Springfield, Va., was in a hay mow, and on descending, jumped several feet, an iron fork penetrated his adbomen several inches. He died 8 days later.

543. Arthur C. W. Reynolds was murdered in a gambling house called Bella Union on December 15th by Reuben Withers of NY City. (Calif. news).

544. The body of Thomas Brown, a sailor, was discovered near the road leading from San Francisco to the Mission, stabbed in 24 places. (Calif. news).

545. Mr. J. G. Mariner died on the 24th of December from the effects of an over dose of laudanum. (Calif. news).

546. Mr. Edward Hitchins, aged 25, of Charlestown, Mass., was drowned Dec 26. (Calif. news).

547. Mr. Adam Story, formerly of Catskill, NY, died in San Francisco on the 23d of December, aged 28 years. (Calif. news).

548. Richard Richards, about 35, and his child, died in a house fire in the town of Marcy, about 2 miles from Joy's tavern. (Utica Observer).

549. At Galveston, Dr. T. F. Mills, brother of John J. Mills, was killed in a duel by Dr. Neale.

February 16, 1850
550. Feb 11, Malden, Asa Biglow, 71, born in Marlboro, Conn.

43

551. Feb 9, Kingston, William James Carson, aged 8 months.

552. Feb 2, Kingston, Mary Emma, infant child of James E. Low.

553. Saturday, drowned in the Hudson River, Charles and George, sons of Thomas D. Coe., of Cold Spring.

554. Friday afternoon last, Dr. John Richard Jones, of Burlington, died due to the accidental discharge of a gun.

555. On the 31st ult., Orange County, Florida, Hannah Coleman, daughter of Frank Coleman, a blacksmith, died when her clothes caught on fire.

556. Michael Daley was burned to death on Friday last, at his home on Ann Street, Boston.

557. The Utica Gazette reports the death of the 5 year old daughter of Mr. Geo. Parson, the owner of a livery stable.

558. James Mc Elroy, an Irishman, was frozen to death in a barn in Hadley, Saratoga county, a few days ago.

559. Gen. Bem, the Hungarian patriot, is reported to have died suddenly in Turkey.

560. Capt. Bursley and 11 of his men died when the packet ship Hottinguer broke up on the Arlow Bank off Wexford. (European news).

561. A woman named O'Brien was found dead near Massasoit Falls, Fall River on Monday evening.

562. Feb 18, Plattekill, at the residence of her grandfather, Margaretta, daughter of Charles and Ann Eliza Brodhead of Kingston, aged 6 years and 4 months.

563. Jeremiah Rogers, died in Calif., a son of David Rogers, and brother to the others whose death we have heretofore published, a short time since. The last male member of that family and the 5th to die there. (Hudson Gazette).

564. Mrs. Hart was instantly killed in New Orleans on the 6th inst.

565. The partners of the late Mr. Stickney, who committed suicide at Boston, have published a card attributing the immediate cause which led to the fatal deed to a disease contracted in California, and to hereditary disposition to insanity.

566. Sarah, wife of Peter Lee, died instantly on Thursday morning, at her residence in Washington street, Hoboken.

567. Lieut. H. Neal, of the US Dragoons, commmitted suicide. (Austin (Tex.) Tel., Jan 24).

568. At Mt. Savage, Md., on Sunday, a Welshman named John Davis was found across the railroad lying dead by exposure whilst under the influence of liquor.

569. Some 3-4 months since, the wife of Ezck Carr died at the town of Westerlo. Her husband is held for the murder.

570. Mr. George Drysdale lost three children and a grandchild in a house fire on the 22nd ult. at Big Tracedie.

March 2, 1850
571. Monday, in this village, George P. Schoonmaker, aged 40.

572. Feb 25, Kingston, Alonzo D. Felter, about 50.

573. Feb 27, Kingston, Adelaide F., daughter of William H. Deforest, aged 5 years, 3 months and 19 days.

574. Feb 2, Acra, Greene County, James Webster, a soldier of the Revolution, in his 91st year.

575. An accident occurred on the 14th section of the Baltimore and Ohio Railroad, about 5 miles above Cresaptown, on the night of Monday the 11th ult., by which two men, Patrick Caray and John Dooley were drowned.

576. On the ship Columbus, during a passage from Liverpool to New York, William Brown fell from the mast and was drowned.

577. Monday, Patroon Street, Albany, Michael Griffin and his horse were killed.

578. Thursday, the 14th ult., Joseph Spencer, about 70, of the town of Friendship, Allegany County, died under unusual circumstances. (Angelica Reporter).

579. Gen. John Mc Neil, late Surveyor of the Port of Boston, died in Washington on Saturday evening.

580. An equestrian named Kelly fell dead from his horse in the ring of Stokes circus at Franklin La. on the 1st. He belonged to Patterson, NJ.

581. Mr. Jenkins, a conductor on the Housatonic Railroad, died recently.

582. A party of Texans, trading to Mexico, was fired upon by the official bandits, and Mr. Worthington, Mr. Campbell and Mr. Bowen were killed.

583. On Monday morning last an inquest was held at Cumberland, Md. over the body of John J. Hickman, found hanging.

584. Mary Ann Mc Gaurren, daughter of John Mc Gaurren, an industrious cooper of Twaalfskill, died of burns on the 19th.

585. We learn from the Ulster Republican that a man named Mc Mannus, of Rondout, was killed by the kick of a horse at Higginsville, in the western part of the village of Kingston, on Tuesday morning. Burial at Rondout.

586. Jan 20, Marion, Ky., William T. Wallingford killed his wife and babe. (Louisville Journal).

March 9, 1850
587. George R. Weitsenger, associate editor and proprietor of the Louisville Journal, died on the 25th ult. of congestion of the brain.

588. On Saturday last, Cornelius Driscoll, about 14, fell from the roof of a three story house in Avenue D, NY and died.

589. Dr. Brown, a physician in Seabrook, aged 45, a widower, committed suicide.

590. Andrew Tears, a resident of Wallkill, Orange county (near Scotchtown) aged 63, hung himself on

46

Tuesday of last week. (Sullivan Whig).

591. The dead body of Mr. Mc Cracken was, on
Friday last, found in a stable in West End,
Alexandria, Va. with a rope around his neck.

592. The Washington Republic says that a white man
named Lubbin was accidently drowned in Rock Creek
on Saturday night.

593. John Pasqual was arrested in Charleston on
Mar 2 for poisoning Mrs. James Rose with arsenic
last summer.

March 16, 1850
594. Mar 10, Kingston, Lovina, wife of Amer
Richardson, aged 31.

595. Mar 3, Kingston, Theodore F. Trempper, aged 3
years, 4 months and 3 days.

596. Mar 11, Kingston, George H., son of Henry and
Nelly Hasbrouck, aged 11 months and 16 days.

597. The Captain May, reported to have died at St.
Louis, was Captain Thomas C. May, formerly of
Pittsburgh.

598. George Byers, of Kittaning, Pa., was killed
on the 21st ult. by the accidental discharge of
his gun while hunting.

599. Gen. Ebenezer Beach, of Rochester, was found
dead in his bed on Wednesday evening. He was the
most extensive miller in the country.

600. All hands lost when the schooner Isabella
foundered off Sandy Hook. Samuel Penny, leaving a
wife and 3 children at 15 Goerck street in this
city; his brother Wm. Penney, the steward, leaving
a wife and 5 children, and the mate Wm. Spencer,
who leaves a young wife to whom he had been
married about 4 months, and three others. (NY
Sun).

601. Monday, as the mid-day freight train from
Troy was going west, when within 6 miles of
Schenectady, the locomotive Boston's boiler burst,
instantly killing Wm. Wiggings, engineer. The
fireman Thomas O'Conner was very seriously injured
and fears are entertained for his recovery.

602. Henry Pullen, of Providence, RI, died on
Sunday morning last, just before we entered
Havana, and was buried at sea. (Calif. news).

603. Rev. Porter Clay, last surviving brother of
the Hon. H. Clay, died in Camden, Arkansas on the
16th ult., in the 71st year of his age.

March 23, 1850
604. Mar 13, Caatsban, Mrs. Anna Rightmyer,
consort of Mr. Wm. Rightmyer, in her 66th year.

605. A man named Carroll was stabbed on Sunday
night in NY, and died on Tuesday.

606. Two men, Starr and Chandler, from Medina,
Orleans county were murdered by Chilians in the
mines of California. (Rochester Advertiser).

607. The Richmond Enquirer says that on Friday of
last week, Mr. Carr, toll gatherer on Mayo's
Bridge, while attempting to rescue his little
daughter, who had fallen into the river, drowned
with her.

608. At the Brooklyn Navy Yard last week, Sergeant
James Montgomery, of the marines, committed
suicide.

609. The Natchez Courier of the 26th ult. says
that a few days previous a boat landed above
Natchez, filled with several families from Murray
county, Ga. Cholera developed itself among them
this side of Vicksburgh and on the 18th ult. a
negro man, belonging to a Mr. Barton, died.
Afterwards Mrs. Sally Barton, Able Barton, son of
James Barton, Eli Gentry, Miss Hannah George, Jane
Gentry, James Green, John Green and Elizabeth
Green, children, Mrs. Elizabeth George and Miss
Minerva Barton, all died.

610. A young man named Wasson, of Perkins Grove,
Bureau county, Ill., was killed by Indians near
California.

March 30, 1850
611. Died in Sommerville, Mass. on the 13th inst.,
Mr. Thos. Rand, aged 90 years. For 70 years he
has assisted in supplying Boston with milk.

612. Mr. Thomas Andrews, for many years a funeral
undertaker in Boston, but never vaccinated, died

48

of small pox on Sunday.

613. Hon. Samuel Adams died in Saline county,
Arkansas on the 27th ult. He had been president
of the Senate, acting governor and state
treasurer.

614. Hon. Charles A. Barnitz, of York Pa., died on
the 8th inst. He was an able lawyer and served
with distinction in Congress.

615. Mr. Alpheus Miller, liquor merchant of
Auburn, came to his death at Waterloo, on Saturday
last, in consequence of drinking too much liquor.
(Seneca Observer).

616. During the recent dreadful catastrophe on the
Mobile river, in the burning of the Orline St.
John, the carpenter of the boat, who had on board
three negroes belonging to himself and his
brother, jumped with the negroes into the yawl
boat and cut her adrift, thus depriving the
passengers and crew of the only means of escape.
The wretch, whose name was Robert Mc Caw, was met
a few days afterwards at Cahawba, and immediately
killed by M. Gale, Pilot of the Orline St. John.

617. From the Rio Grande, an account of the murder
of Mr. St. John Luke, a well known musician, which
took place on the 3d inst., has been received.

618. Johnston, convicted of the murder of Judge
Van Winkle, near Patterson, NJ, has been sentenced
to be executed on the 30th of April next.

April 6, 1850
619. The Jacksonville (Ala.) Republican contains
an obituary notice for John Chandler, who died
near that place on the 13th ult., aged 104. He
served in the Revolutionary war for 7 years under
Generals Greene and Sumter and at the battles of
Eutaw, Camden and Cowpens.

620. On the 12th inst., Mr. Gerrit Brown, of
Pharsalia, received an injury while chopping in
the woods, which caused his death in 36 hours. He
leaves a wife and 5 children.

621. Ezekiel Webster, elder brother of Daniel
Webster, died in April, 1829 at Concord.

622. Francis Blackney died in the wreck of the steamer Wilson G. Hunt, says the Bermuda Gazette of the 12th. (NY Evening Post).

April 13, 1850

623. Apr 6, in this village, of consumption, S. P., wife of H. W. France, aged 38 years, 9 months and 6 days.

624. Apr 6, in this village, Catharine, widow of the late Capt. George Taylor, about 58.

625. Apr 6, in this village, James Oakley, son of Thomas Van Keuren, 1 year old.

626. Apr 11, in this town, Maria, wife of Tobias Wynkoop, Esq., about 56.

627. The wife of William Coir of Batavia, on Monday of last week, swallowed two teaspoonsful of corrosive sublimate (thinking it laudanum) to cure the toothache, and died from the effects very soon after.

628. The English papers announce the death of Sir Wm. Allen, an artist, at the age of 68.

629. The wife of Senator Dawson, of Georgia, died Monday morning at the United States Hotel in Washington.

630. The Hon. James Emott died on Saturday morning last in his 80th year. (Poughkeepsie Telegraph).

631. Deacon Samuel Eaton, of Plaistow, NH, formerly toll keeper of the Haverill Bridge, was killed on Monday of last week.

632. Mr. Charles Edwards, a citizen of Delhi, committed suicide on Saturday last. (Gazette).

633. Mr. Wilson, from NY, was married at Washington city on Wednesday evening and found dead in his bed beside his bride on Thursday morning.

April 20, 1850

634. Apr 12, Kingston, James Cassel, about 60.

635. Apr 14, Kingston, John Harris, about 44.

636. Apr 14, Kingston, the wife of Egbert
Elmendorf, about 46.

637. Apr 9, Kingston, Melissa A., daughter of
William Scofield, aged 10 years and 11 months.

638. Two sons of S. Johnson, one 12 the other 14,
were killed in the gun-powder explosion at the
Andover Mine in Sussex, NJ on Tuesday of last
week.

639. Mr. Richello, a tavern-keeper, living about 8
miles from Richmond, Va., was murdered on Saturday
night last.

640. John Ryan, an Irishman, was walking by the
side of the Western Railroad track near Warren on
Saturday evening last. He was struck by the train
from Boston.

641. A rencountre occurred at Mobile, Alabama on
the 5th between David White and Henry M. Jackson,
in which both fired pistols and White was shot
dead.

642. Gad N. Chapin, a mechanic engaged in the
Cotton Mills at Moravia, Cayuga county, was killed
on Wednesday last.

643. Mr. James Lee, second engineer of the steamer
Fanny, was accidently killed below New Orleans on
the 15th by the falling of a crank.

644. Henry Clay was 73 years old on the 12th
inst., having been born on the 12th day of April
1777.

645. John Maree, a young man, formerly employed by
the Western Telegraph Office in Baltimore,
committed suicide on Sunday last.

646. Mr. Henry Bear, of Montgomery county, O.,
committed suicide the other day by hanging himself
with a grape vine.

647. John Mc Bean, formerly bar-keeper on board
the steamer Vesta, was found dead on the Levee in
New Orleans.

648. On Friday of last week, the 12 year old son
of Mr. Alanson Bune of Centreport, LI, was killed
in the grist mill belonging to the estate of

Joseph C. Lewis.

649. The wife of Hon. Noble S. Elderkin, Speaker
of the Assembly, died at Potsdam on the 8th inst.,
aged 38.

650. Mr. John B. Rust, pilot of the steamboat New
York, was instantly killed yesterday by being
caught in the machinery. (NY Mirror).

651. Major O'Brien, an army officer who served
with distinction at the Battle of Buena Vista,
died in Indianola, Texas on the 30th, of cholera.

April 27, 1850
652. Sunday last, Kingston, of dropsy, Herman M.
Romeyn, in his 58th year.

653. Apr 13, Windham Center, Josiah Brainerd, aged
76.

654. On Wednesday of last week, a child of Mr.
Alexander Salpagh, of Hudson, aged about 18
months, was so dreadfully burnt in consequence of
its clothes taking fire that it lived but a few
hours.

655. Francis Tompkins, colored, was found murdered
in the Patchoque woods on Friday of last week,
having been killed by a fellow woodman, Joseph
Benjamen, who has disappeared.

656. In the murder case at Saco, the Coroner's
Jury returned a verdict in the effect that
deceased, whose name is Mary Bain, came to her
death from drugs administered and instruments used
by Dr. James H. Smith, in an attempt to procure
abortion.

657. G. W. Ragsdale, clerk of the US District
Court of Miss., was killed by a gun loaded with
buckshot at Pontotoe, Miss., lately.

658. On March 27th, Don Juan de Dios Canedo, a
Deputy of Congress was assassinated in his own
house in the city of Mexico.

659. A little daughter of Mr. Davis, of Darian,
Ct., was burned to death recently.

660. The death of Mr. Grinnell (father of the
member of Congress of that name, and of the Hon.

Moses H. Grinnell, of N. York) is announced at New
Bedford, Mass. Also the death of Mr. Roach, a
merchant of New Bedford.

661. We learn with deep regret that Isaac L.
Hasbrouck, Esq., of High Falls, in this county,
has been seriously injured in an explosion on
Wednesday of last week, so that his recovery will
be a marvel.

662. A little girl, aged 4, daughter of the Peake
family of singers, was burned to death on the 19th
in Medford, Mass.

663. Wm. K. Gardiner and Henry Humphrey, captain
and first mate of the brig Francis Jean, were
charged with causing the death of David Thompson,
a colored man.

                    May 4, 1850
664. Apr 28, Mariette, daughter of Evert Wynkoop,
Esq., in her 21st year.

665. Apr 27, Kingston, Jane Catherine, wife of
Wessel Ten Brouck, aged 33.

666. Apr 14, Kingston, Helen, wife of Egbert
Elmendorf, aged 52.

667. Mrs. Ireland and her daughter, of Quincy,
Ill., came to an awful death by freezing and
starvation on the mountains during the past
winter. They were on their way to California. A
husband survived.

668. Charles Humphrey, of Ithaca, Tompkins county,
died at Albany on the 17th of April, aged 59.

669. Michael Keaty was instantly killed by the
caving in of a bank of earth in Albany last week.

670. The Charleston papers of the 27th are filled
with the details of the funeral honors paid to the
remains of Mr. Calhoun.

671. Lost in the explosion of the Wayne on Lake
Erie, Mr. J. Ellore, 1st engineer and Mr. Edward
Buchard, 2nd engineer.

672. Herman M. Romeyn died in Kingston on Sunday
last, aged 60, says the Sullivan Whig. (Rondout
Courier).

673. Apr 28, in this town, Tjerck Osterhoudt, aged 56.

674. May 1, Kingston, Brainerd, only son of James S. and Sarah M. Pine, aged 10 months, 12 days.

675. Mar 7, Kingston, Lee L., youngest son of Geo. and Harriet Mc Kown, aged 1 year, 12 days.

676. Apr 26, Rochester, Jane, consort of William Greene, aged 72.

677. Died in Scituate, Mass., on the 22nd ult., Mr. Simeon Pincin, 97. His wife, who survives, is 102, married 75 years.

678. In Cincinnati, on the 1st inst., Frederick Fritz committed suicide.

679. Mrs. Case, an estimable lady of Montgomery county, Md., a day or two since, became the mother of three children and, unfortunately, died in giving birth to the fourth.

680. Rev. Cyrus Barker, missionary to Assam (E. I.) under the patronage of the Baptist Missionary Union, died of consumption Jan 31st and was buried in Mozambique channel.

681. James Mc Can, Jr., convicted of the murder of Joseph Toland, was hung near Columbus, Miss., on the 19th ultimo.

682. William Barber, aged about 23, son of Orbin Barber, was accidently thrown from a raft on Wednesday last, in the east branch of the Delaware river, in the town of Colchester, and drowned.

683. In March last, Mrs. Gerry House, of Maine, died.

684. On the 2d, an inquest upon the body of Alexander Wilson, picked up in the Rondout Creek near Eddyville. An Englishman, about 40, with a family, he fell from a small boat and was drowned on the 22d.

685. On the 26th ult., a dreadful accident occurred at Ulsterville, in the scythe factory of Mr. France. Thomas Schoonmaker, an operative in the factory, was killed by the bursting of a

grindstone while in motion.

686. Lieut. Penderhurst has died of yellow fever
in Rio Janeiro.

687. Orrin Vreddenberg, of Philadelphia, and A.
Dickerman, of Clinton Co., Iowa, were killed by
the caving of a bank under which they were at
work, at Mormon Island, on the 17th of March.
(Calif. news).

688. In Stillwater, Minn., a boy named Mc Millen,
12, was sentenced to one year in prison, 20 days
in solitary, for killing his schoolmate, Herman
Snow.

689. On Friday of last week, at New Haven, James
M. Caffrey, convicted of the murder of Mrs. Ann
Smith, was sentenced to be hung on the 2d of
October, next.

May 18, 1850
690. At Belleville, La., on the 20th ult.,
Bartholemew Mullen murdered Patrick Downes.

691. A 12-13 year old son of Mr. Hodge, of
Napanoch, drowned on Monday last. (Ellenville
Journal).

692. The Charleston papers records the death, on
the 9th inst., of Judge Richardson, aged 73.

693. Miss Eliza Mc Dowell, of Alleghany township,
Blair county, Pa., committed suicide on Tuesday
evening last.

694. Braxton Meeks drowned while intoxicated at
Hagerstown, Md.

695. Last week, Mrs. Crozier died in Halifax, Vt.,
at the extraordinary age of 107.

696. Henry Gunn, a slave, charged with having
murdered his master, Mr. R. Wichello, was
convicted and will be hung on the 25th of June.

May 25, 1850
697. Mar 1, Sacramento City, Calif., of chronic
dysentary, William, son of Robert Dorlan of
Catskill, about 22.

698. May 15, Kingston, Elizabeth Van Aken, wife of Henry Van Aken, aged 25 years, 1 month and 17 days.

699. May 15, Kingston, William Hamilton, aged 41 years, 6 months and 10 days.

700. May 21, Kingston, Elizabeth Ennis, wife of Joseph Ennis, aged 23 years, 11 months and 21 days.

701. May 13, Rondout, Sarah E., only child of John and Ann Eliza Vandemark, aged 2 years and 1 month.

702. Two brothers named Cooper, and a boy named Slack, were drowned in the Schuylkill above Columbia Bridge, Philadelphia, on Sunday the 9th inst, by the upsetting of a boat.

703. John Sixsmith, Sen. was charged with killing a youth named William Hyland at Hardings, Phila. on Monday the 13th inst.

704. On Friday afternoon, Henry Franklin, an only and very promising son of Mr. Isaac S. Clough, of Waltham, Mass., fell into the Common Pond and drowned.

705. Ellen Collins, residing in Front St., Newburgh, was murdered on Saturday, May 11th, by her step son.

706. In Nashua, May 15th, a man named J. Hart Allen, about 50, murdered his little girl, about 2, then went into a privy and humg himself.

707. Mr. Wright Wilson, overseer on the plantation of Mr. Hobgood, in the parish of De Sota, La., while endeavoring to correct a negro slave for some fault, on the 27th ult., was stabbed in 36 places by the negro, killing him almost instantly. The negro committed suicide and another was shot.

708. An inquest was held on Monday, at the foot of Harrison st., NY on the body of Patrick Wallace, a native of Ireland, about 36, found drowned in the North River. In his pocket was a letter from his wife dated at Rallagh, Ireland, March 11, 1850.

709. John Leonard, a hack driver, who resided at No. 196 Duane street, NY, committed suicide on

Saturday night.

710. From a letter, dated Canton, Feb 25, Taukwang, or Glory of Reason, the Emperor of China is dead. He is the second son of Kiaking and the sixth of the Tsing or Manchan dynasty which has reigned over the celestial empire since 1644. Taukwang ascended the dragon's throne in 1821, and has reigned 29 years. His age is 69.

711. Ten deaths in Galveston during the week of the 10th inst. Mr. A. Bond, a stranger named Welles and a sailor. The rest were children. (from Texas, New Orleans Crescent).

June 1, 1850

712. May 22, Poughkeepsie, Moses Clement, printer, aged 81.

713. Baron Menneval, the well known Private Secretary of the Emperor Napoleon, died lately in Paris, aged 73.

714. A fire-man on the Utica and Schenectady Rail-road named Joseph Myres, was killed instantly on Thursday week, at Ferguson's Bridge, three miles below Utica.

715. A murder was committed lately in the Swedish colony in Henry Co., Ill. A man named Root deliberatly shot Johnson the Prophet. Root's wife had joined the colony, which accounts for his anger.

716. Jonathan B. Pratt of Worcester, Mass., was discovered floating in the water on the morning of the 19th, at the dock at Kingston (Jam.). He was a passengers on the Crescent City, (Calif. news).

717. Mr. Stephen Wilson, 28, son of Mr. William Wilson of Poughkeepsie, committed suicide at Stockton. (Calif. news).

718. Asa and Henry F. Wentworth, who are charged with the murder of Jonas Parker, at Manchester, have been given up by the Governor of Maine.

June 8, 1850

719. The Rev. John Newland Maffit died suddenly in Mobile on the 25th ult.

720. Stephen Denman, of Grahamsville, Sull. Co.,
was killed in the woods on the 23d ult. by the
falling of a tree.

721. Commodore Cooper died on Saturday at his
residence in Willow street, Brooklyn, at the age
of about 57 years.

722. Senator Elmore, of SC, who was appointed to
fill the vacancy in the US Senate produced by the
death of John C. Calhoun, died suddenly at
Washington on the 29th of May. His disease was
bronchial consumption and erysipelas.

                      June 15, 1850
723. Jun 10, in this village, Ellen Augusta,
daughter of William and Catharine Krows, in her
13th year.

724. Jun 3, Kingston, Benjamin, son of Samuel and
Hannah Styles, aged 17.

725. Jun 2, Clinton, Dutchess Co., of consumption,
John Mc Caby, aged 44.

726. Jun 3, in the town of Rochester, Richard
Munson, aged 56.

727. Jun 6, Wilbur, Michael, son of John Dunn,
aged 14.

728. Jun 2, Poughkeepsie, Mrs. Mary Newman
Tallman, wife of John B. Tallman, Esq., aged 33.

729. May 24, Wawarsing, Lydia Maria, wife of Louis
Schuster, aged 24.

730. Jun 2, Wawarsing, Anna, wife of Wilhelmus
Bevier, aged 79.

731. May 29, Port Benjamin, Wawarsing, Cornelia
Ann, wife of John Decker, in her 22nd year.

732. Information has been transmitted to the State
Department from the US Consul at Kingston,
announcing the death of Messrs. J. B. Pratt and
Abner Marlton, bound to Chagres, from New York, in
the steamship Crescent City.

733. Jacob Myers, about 9, met with his death
yesterday by falling into the 'hopper' at the
steam plaster mill near the state dam. (Troy

Budget).

734. M. M. Robinson, Esq., formerly editor of the Richmond Compiler (now Times) died in New Orleans on the 30th ult.

735. About one o'clock on the afternoon of the 10th inst., J. T. Brinham, Esq., expired.

736. The body of Robert J. Buckley, employed as an engineer on a plantation on the Island of Cuba, was found dead in the streets on the 15th of November, 1849, supposed to have been murdered. His mother and sister reside in either Dutchess or Ulster County. (Poughkeepsie American).

737. Wm. D. Hammond was convicted at Columbia, SC for the murder of his father. He will be hung on the 12th of July next.

June 22, 1850
738. On Friday night, David Johnson, about 21, an Irishman and a hand on board one of the Albany barges lying at the foot of Clinton st., drowned.

739. William Gillespie, a cousin to the gallant Gillespie who fell at the storming on Monterey, was killed on the 29th ultimo in an Indian battle. (Corpus Christi Nueces Valley of the 1st inst.).

740. David Boston, a colored man, died near Rochester, Md. on the 1st inst., from the effects of superstition. (Balt. Sun).

741. A wealthy farmer by the name of Gay, living near Stockport Landing, Columbia county, strangled himself by placing his neck between the branches of a tree in his orchard on Thursday week.

742. Cecily, a negress, was hung on Friday the 24th for the murder of Dr. Longgon, his wife and child. (Paulding Clarion, 25th).

743. Dateline, Buffalo, Jun 18. In the fire on board the Griffith the following were killed: Capt. Roby, wife and daughter; Michael Juno, 3rd engineer; Mr. Mann, wheelsman; Mr. Traley, first porter; Messrs. Tillum and Poulding, saloon keepers; the wife and child of Wm. Tinckon; R. S. Parks of Beaver, Pa.; C. Leonard, porter; D. Weaver, waiter; Mrs. Wilkinson and daughters of J. Chapman. The number saved was 40, about 250 lost.

(Albany Eve. Journal).

June 29, 1850

744. Mrs. Maria Hester, wife of Samuel L. Gouverneur, Esq., and daughter of the late President Monroe, died at Oak Hill, London County, Va., on the 20th inst.

745. William Champlin, aged 20, in the employ of Mr. David Porter, of Schoharie, was drowned while bathing in Schoharie Creek, near that place, on Sunday last. He has left a mother and two brothers who reside at 103 Seventeenth st., NY.

746. The dwelling house of Mr. John Palmer, about 4 miles from Rome, Oneida County, on the Hampton road, was struck by lightning on Thursday and Mr. Richard East, who was white-washing in the lower part of the house was instantly killed.

747. Jacob Hays, the veteran High Constable of New York, died in that city on Friday week, in the 79th year of his age.

748. Mathew L. Davis, of NY, died Friday week at the residence of his son in Manhattanville.

749. William Gardner and William Humphries were convicted of manslaughter at Baltimore, in the death of David Thomas, cook on the brig Francis Jane.

750. Esek Carr was acquitted of manslaughter in the recent death of his wife. (Albany Argus).

July 6, 1850

751. Jul 2, Flatbush, John L. Osterhoudt, about 35.

752. A little son of Mr. Geo. R. Freeman, of Nashua, 4 years old, died on Monday of last week of hydrophobia. (NH Telegraph).

753. The widow Sarah Welsh, aged 101, died in Boston on Thursday last. A native of Gloucester and daughter of Jonathan Coates. To be interred at Newburyport. (Traveller).

754. Mrs. Bird, of Hudson, NH, was burned to death on the 26th ult. by her clothes catching fire.

755. George Dolton and Hiram Fetter were suffocated by the foul air of a well they were cleaning at Clintock's Hill, Alleghany City, Pa., on Thursday of last week.

756. Mr. John Morrison, of Saxonville, was found dead on Sunday morning last in Cochituate brook, near its junction with the Concord river, in Saxonville, Mass.

757. Three gentlemen left Moro on the 19th of May. On their arrival at Wagon Mound, about 118 miles from Santa Fe, they found the following Express bearers dead: Frank Hendrickson, James Clay, --- Brenton, John Williams, a teamster; Thomas Flournoy, a merchant, formerly, it is believed, of Lexington; Benjamin Shaw, a Santa Fe merchant; John Duty, Moses Goldstien and John Freeman. (from the Plains).

758. Two boys, Ira Shook, aged 15 and Nelson Lynch, 18, were killed by lightning on the 20th ult. in Waterloo, NY.

759. General Zachary Huntington died on Sunday afternoon last at 86 years of age, a respected citizen of Norwich. (Norwich (Ct.) Couree).

July 13, 1850
760. Jun 30, Kingston, Hannah, wife of Abel Patterson, aged 32 years and 6 months.

761. Jul 5, Rochester, Esther Krom, aged 74.

762. Wm. Shean, prefect of Georgetown College, was drowned in the Potomac on Friday week.

763. Mr. Wm. Phean, the prefect of Georgetown College (DC) was accidently drowned in the Potomac on the 4th inst.

764. Rev. Alexander Danoon died at Caledonia, Monroe Co., NY on the 17th ult., at the age of 80.

765. S. S. Prentiss, lawyer, formerly of Vicksburgh, and recently of New Orleans, died the other day at Natchez, Miss.

766. On the Fourth of July afternoon, a young lady named Jane Barret, of Phil., was drowned in the river Schuylkill near Manayunk.

767. On the 4th, at New Haven, Norah Welch, aged 10, was killed by running before a cannon at the instant of discharge, and having the upper part of her head carried away.

768. General Zachary Taylor, 12th President of the US, expired Tuesday evening of cholera morbus which passed into bilious remittant fever.

769. Mr. Parks, of Newburyport, who has been missing for two months, was found dead on Friday last.

July 20, 1850
770. Jun 26, in this town, Mrs. Catherine Crawford, consort of Rev. John Crawford, about 75.

771. Jul 16, in this village, Miss Elizabeth Knapp, aged 23.

772. Jul 16, in this town, Paul Lasher, about 33.

773. Jul 16, Woodstock, Col. John Reynolds, about 35, committed suicide, leaving a family.

774. A letter in the Buffalo Republican announces the death by drowning on the 28th of April in the Yuba river, of Peter Mc Kay and George Barnett. The latter, it is said, leaves a wife and child near Hudson.

775. Lieut. Mason was drowned on the 22d of May in the Rio Grande.

776. Mr. Abraham Tourtelot was killed in Clarksville, Conn. by lightning, during the severe storm of last Friday night.

777. Rev. Edward L. Parker, of Derry, NH, died on Sunday evening, 14th.

778. Hon. Nathaniel Silsbee, of Salem, Mass., died at his residence on the 15th.

779. Lieut. J. Griffin was upset in a sailing boat, opposite Albany, on the 16th, and drowned.

780. James Johnson, a colored man, committed suicide Friday morning by plunging into the Rondout Creek. (Rondout Courier).

781. The 6 year old son of Mrs. Parsons, a widow
of this village, drowned on Thursday near
Williams' ship yard. (Rondout Courier).

782. On Saturday last, George Melvin, 22, of
Ellenville was killed at Port Jervis. (Rondout
Courier).

783. Zachary Taylor was born in Orange county, Va.
in 1784.

July 27, 1850
784. Jul 19, Rondout, Rufus Palen, son of Hiram
and Lamira E. Roosa, 1 year, 10 months and 19 days
old.

785. Jul 6, Wawarsing, James I. Bruyn, aged 66.

786. Jul 8, Honesdale, Pa., at the home of his son
Russell F. Lord, Zelotus Lord, about 60.

787. Jul 18, Marbletown, of consumption, Lewis
Wygant, about 49.

788. Edward Thompson, of Port Colden, was drowned
in Lehigh, near Easton, on Thursday week, while
attempting to save others.

789. Presidential statistics: George Washington
died on Dec 14, 1799 in his 68th year. John Adams
died on Jul 4, 1826. Thomas Jefferson died on Jul
4, 1826 in his 86th year. James Madison died on
Jun 28, 1836 in his 86th year. John Q. Adams died
on Feb 23, 1848. General Andrew Jackson died on
Jun 8, 1845. General W. H. Harrison died on Apr 4,
1841 at Washington in his 69th year. General
Taylor died on Jul 8, 1850. (Washington Union).

790. The ship Elizabeth, from the Mediterannean,
went on shore off Fire Island on Friday. Lost
were Margaret Fuller, her husband and child and
Mr. Henry Sumner of Boston.

August 3, 1850
791. Jul 30, in this town, of consumption, Mrs.
Altie Kimble, daughter of Hezekiah Wynkoop, Esq.
of Saugerties, in her 50th year.

792. Jul 29, in this village, George, son of Hugh
and Margaret Smith, aged 6 months and 16 days.

793. Jul 29, in this village, at the residence of her father Thomas Keys, of consumption, Margaret, wife of Hugh Smith, aged 27.

794. Aug 2, of consumption, Mr. Benjamin Myer, church services at Caatsban.

795. Nathan Horton, about 20, son of Hiram Horton (deceased) was thrown from a load of hay near Circleville, Orange Co. on Monday last, and died. (Sullivan Whig).

796. Mr. James D. Hall, of Boston, died there on Friday last, from taking corrosive sublimate, given to him by an apothecary, in mistake for calomel.

797. J. L. Wright, Esq., a grocer, died a few days since in that city. (Detroit Free Press).

798. A man named Angevine Titus, 15, fell into a basin near the Columbia street bridge, and drowned. Ebenezer Mc Gee, 24, a resident of this city, fell from a canal boat near Hamilton street bridge, and was also drowned. (Alb. Argus).

799. A young man by the name of Joseph W. Wade, in the employ of Mr. Isaiah Van Kleeck, of this village, about 18, died very suddenly yesterday morning. (Fishkill Standard).

800. On the Erie Railroad on Wednesday, between Narrowsburgh and Lacawaxen, a bridge fell. Killed were Mr. Henry C. Clapp, 19, in charge of sheep and swine, from Menton, Ohio, nephew of Alex. Campbell of Bethany College, Va. and Mr. Bondall, in charge of cattle, from Corning, NY. (NY Evening Post).

801. Mr. John Hart, of Philadelphia, of whom we made mention last week as being seriously injured, died on Saturday last.

802. Francis Dillaway, a housewright, coommitted suicide on Thursday afternoon in the belfrey of Chancey Place Church, Boston.

August 10, 1850

803. Aug 5, Hudson, Ann, wife of James Woodruff, Esq., in her 67th year, leaving a husband and son.

804. Aug 2, Flatbush, Abram I. Burhans, aged 83.

805. Captain Dumont, one of the survivors of the melancholy shipwreck of the Medusa, died a short time since in France, in his 76th year.

806. James Gregg Wilson died a few days since, aged 41.

807. The interment of the remains of the late Commodore Jacob Jones, US Navy took place on Wednesday evening from the residence of Dr. Thomas Dillard, USN, West Chesnut street, Philadelphia. Jones was born in Smyrna, Del. in 1770.

808. On Wednesday evening of last week Margaret Rikert, 18, sister-in-law to W. Cure, inn-keeper in the western part of the village of Kingston, drowned in the Esopus Creek near the Kingston bridge. She was from Rhinebeck.

809. Thomas Haddick was drowned in the Esopus Creek, in the town of Kingston, on the 25th ult.

810. On Friday last, two Americans were murdered in their tent at Jamestown, Mr. Chase of New Bedford and Mr. Hathaway of Dighton, Mass. (Calif. news).

August 17, 1850
811. Aug 4, Plattekill, Jane Myer, widow of Peter B. Myer, aged 74 years and 11 days.

812. Aug 10, town of Kingston, William E. Schepmoes, in his 40th year.

813. The Springfield Republican of Saturday last records the death of the only daughter and eldest child of Mr. Bancroft, late US Minister to the Court of St. James, aged 17.

814. A fatal affray occurred in Tippah county, Miss. on the 23rd ult. between Drs. Wooten and Brannon. The latter was killed and the former mortally wounded. Cause supposed to arise from prejudices existing between them, one being a botanical and the other a mineral physician.

815. In Greenwood, La., lately, a fight took place between two young men named Hamilton and Lee, in which Hamilton was killed by five stabs with a knife.

816. Theobald Scharr and John Scharr, workmen engaged in the building of Messrs. Seltzer & Hammer's powder mill on Mill Creek near St. Clair, Schuylkill county, were killed in an explosion on Monday last. Two lads, one 17 the other 10, sons of Mr. Solomon Mc Kinney of Barry township were also killed, as was Mr. Daniel Dengler of Barry. (Pottsville Emporium).

August 24, 1850

817. Sunday last, Shandaken, John Artman, of this village, aged 67.

818. Mrs. Backus, a lady from Boston, was riding with friends near Rochester and fell from the carriage. She died on Saturday morning.

819. John W. Rumph, of the town of Crawford, Orange county, lost his life on the 6th inst. by falling from a bridge at Searsburgh.

820. John Coleman, a boy, was shot at Richmond on Aug 19, by another boy named Jesse Irvin.

821. A man named Schoneman of Sheneman, a merchant tailor of Philadelphia, was drowned at Cape May on the 18th inst.

822. We regret to learn that Mr. Frederick Seymore, long known as attached to the firm of Merrill, Duele and Co., of NY, was drowned near Alburgh Springs on Tuesday the 6th inst.

823. William A. Caldwell, of Whitehall, 26-30 and Louisa C. Van Winkle, also known of late as Knapp, 25-30 and stated to be from Brooklyn, were both found dead at the St. Charles Hotel in Troy on Wednesday. She had her throat cut, he a suicide.

824. Joseph Hall, seaman on the Philadelphia, fell overboard on the 16th of July. (Calif. news).

825. Arthur Hawkins, seaman on the Philadelphia, died suddenly of congestion of the brain, caused by being overheated, on the 17th July. (Calif. news).

826. Boston, Aug 19th, on Friday a party of five persons consisting of Captain Samuel Fuller and his son, of Rockport, Mr. Greig, a lad named Ingles of Brooklyn, NY and Francis E. De Blois, of this city, went on a fishing excursion, and are

supposed to have all been drowned in the capsizing
of the boat in a squall. The bodies of Capt.
Fuller and Mr. Greig have been recovered, also the
jacket of De Blois.

827. From the Boston Traveller, dateline
Lynnfield, Aug 15: A painful casualty occurred
this afternoon in the Suntang Lake, in this town.
Drowned include Robert Shirtliff and wife
Elizabeth Shirtliff, who had been married but a
short time, Catherine L. Adams, Mrs. Mary Howard,
Mary Augusta Howard, two children of Mr. Ephraim
Brown, Mrs. Mehitable Alley, wife of Mr. Jacob
Alley, Miss A. Johnson, Miss Young, a daughter of
Mr. Washington Alley, Marie Cheever and two
children of Mr. Joshua Garland.

828. John W. Webster will be hung on Friday, the
30th inst., in Boston, for the murder of Dr.
Parkman.

829. Hon. B. F. Butler will pronounce a eulogy
upon Hon. Silas Wright at Weybridge, Vt. on the
27th inst.

830. A convict named Wat died of cholera at the
Indiana penitentiary.

August 31, 1850
831. Aug 27, Palenville, William H. Cole, aged 23
years, 11 months.

832. Aug 24, in this village, Jane, daughter of
David and Margaret Hopkins, in her 6th year.

833. George Budd, the well known musical amateur,
is dead.

834. Dr. Blake, surgeon of the 20th regiment now
in garrison at Montreal, deprived himself of his
life on Friday of last week, by cutting his throat
with a razor.

835. A fatal affair occurred at Louisville on the
28th, at a house of ill fame, when a man named
Figg shot Lizzie Schermerhorn, an inmate, and then
shot himself with the same pistol. He died soon
afterwards and the woman is not expected to
recover.

836. Thursday, in this town, Mr. William Myer, about 75, funeral from the Dutch Reformed Church.

837. Aug 27, Palenville, William H. Coon, aged 23 years, 11 months.

838. Tragedy at Louisville, a man named John Figg attemted to kill a girl at a house of common resort in Lafayette st. on the 28th ult. by shooting her in the side. He afterward shot himself through the heart. He had been a lover of the girl, who was 18. Her wound is probably fatal.

839. A party of Capt. French's company were attacked by a party of twenty-five Indians, about 60 miles from Corpus Christi, and two of the party, namely Sullivan and Wilbargen were killed.

840. Funeral services were performed on Friday evening of last week by Rev. Dr. Walker, at the residence of Mrs. Webster in Cambridge. The remains of Professor Webster were conveyed by Mr. John Peake, undertaker, to Mount Auburn and deposited in the family vault.

841. A brother of Jesse Hammond, of Kingston, was drowned in the Hudson, on Monday Aug 26th, opposite Hyde Park. (Rondout Courier, 30th).

842. John Inman, late editor of the NY Commercial Advertiser, died on Friday week, aged 47 years, brother of Henry Inman, painter.

843. A man named Potter, a mason, aged 50, belonging to Topsfield, and his son, aged 8, while crossing Ipswich marshes, on Monday morning week, sunk to their necks in mud or bog, and there stuck fast until the tide came up and drowned them.

844. James Donavan was crushed to death at Springfield, Mass. between two cars on Saturday. He leaves a large family.

845. Alexander Hale, in his 24th year, son of Nathan Hale, and editor or the Boston Daily Advertiser, was drowned near Pensacola while attempting to rescue persons from a wreck.

846. The wife of Hon. Josiah Quincy, senior, died at their country residence in Quincy on Saturday,

aged 80.

847. Lieut. Crawley, of the US Navy, died in Charleston on the 15th ult.

848. Last week, a freight train on the Hartford Railroad cut off the leg of a little daughter of Mr. Prior of Windsor Locks, Conn. She died the next day.

849. Mrs. Hannah Secord murdered Mary Ann Smith near Fishkill and died herself on Saturday last of self inflicted wounds.

850. On Saturday, Springfield, Cyrus W. Symonds fell from a window and died.

September 14, 1850
851. Sep 4, Stockbridge, Mass., Robert Watts, Esq., formerly of Westchester Co., NY, aged 66.

852. Sep 6, in this town, John Mc Cormick, 75.

853. Louis Phillippe died on the 26th ult. at Claremount, England, in his 77th year.

854. The president of the Royal Academy, Sir Martin Archer Shee, F. R. S., died on the 19th ult. at Brighton, aged 80.

855. The express train from the West ran off the track at Green's Corner, 20 miles west of Utica, Sep 8th. John Dunn, the fireman, was instantly killed.

856. The steamship Isaac Newton, on her way up the river on Monday night, when off West Point, ran down the sloop Samuel Gordon. The owner Samuel Colman, aged 26, was drowned.

857. On Sunday last, a large funeral procession followed the remains of John Mc Cormick through the village.

858. Morgan Ackert, of Rhinebeck, attempted to jump from the steamboat Armenia on Thursday last at the Kingston landing. He missed the dock and was drowned.

859. Monday night, on the Boston Railroad, the train from Albany had an accident. Dead include: Col. S. G. Mumford, a lawyer of NYC; Miss Jane

Roessle, of Albany, daughter of the proprietor of
the Delevan House and Mr. Whitmore, of Leicester,
Mass.

860. Bishop Bascomb, a famous preacher of the
Methodist Church, died at Louisville on the 9th
ult.

September 21, 1850

861. Sep 17, Napanoch, Mrs. Mary S., wife of Wm.
B. Bange, Esq., aged 24.

862. Thursday, in this town, Abram Newkirk, about
38.

863. Friday, in this town, Charles Vernal, about
40.

864. The Poughkeepsie American says, a man named
De Groff was found dead in the pond below the
Rocky Glen Factory, in the town of Fishkill, on
the morning of the 13th, his body badly bruised
and broken.

865. "Tom Finny", notorious gambler was killed in
Boone Co., Ky. a short time ago.

866. Chuck-a-pe, or Big Haw, head chief of the
Ottoes, died on the 23d and was buried on the
south side of the Platta. (St. Louis, Mo.,
Intelligencer, 5th).

867. Isaac Vosburgh, of Canaan, in attempting to
jump upon a train of cars at Chatham 4 Corners, on
Wednesday week, just as they had started, slipped
and was dragged under the cars, and so severely
injured that he lived but half an hour.

868. Hon. Henry Phinney, President of the Otsego
Bank, and one of the oldest citizens of
Cooperstown, died on Saturday of cholera morebus.

869. Maj. James Bonel, who was engaged in
secreting the stores &c. of the Americas at
Concord, Mass. on the 19th of August 1775, died in
that town last Thursday at the age of 90.

870. Captain Hawley, of the schooner Henry, of
Baltimore, died on Wednesday night at Savannah.

871. A son of Mr. Chauncy Burdevin, of Hudson,
aged about 6 years, was drowned on the 10th inst.

70

872. Jonathan Maltby, the oldest inhabitant of New Haven, died at Fair Haven on Saturday morning, in his 92nd year. A graduate of Yale College, class of 1779.

873. A murderer named Uzza Robbins was executed at Southport, Va. on the 30th of August.

874. Melchoir Belzhoover was killed by an Irishman named Mc Coy about 4 miles from Pittsburg on the 10th inst.

875. At Quincy Point, near Boston, on Friday morning, the son of Mr. Wm. H. Davis was burned to death.

876. Mr. John Morly, of Van Buren, Onondaga Co., died from being kicked by a horse.

September 28, 1850
877. Sep 23, NYC, Adeline, wife of Henry N. Beers, and daughter of the late Asa Bieglow of Malden, in her 27th year.

878. Sep 20, Kingston, Henry Ten Broeck, aged 71 years, 8 months and 23 days.

879. Sep 21, Kingston, Sarah Elizabeth, child of William Hudler, aged 1 year and 6 months.

880. Andrew Brand, the Kentucky Fat Boy, died at Albany on Wednesday morning weighing 537 pounds. He was a native of the town of Calhoun, Davis county, Ky. in his 16th year.

881. The wife of Mr. Carson Bryant of the town of Java, Genessee county, cut the throats of her two youngest children, 3 and 6 months, then committed suicide.

882. Ira Clark, farmer of Orange, Conn., was found dead in a field near his home on Wednesday of last week.

883. Samuel K. Dingle, late Leader of the NY Brass Band, committed suicide on the 18th inst. by hanging himself.

884. James Fowler, who lately died in New Orleans, worth an estate of a million dollars, leaves three sisters in Washington.

885. On the passage of the steamship Ohio from New Orleans by way of Havana, William Field of Providence, RI, Albert Spencer of East Greenwich, George Howell of Sag Harbor and Captain Ira Gould of Huntington, LI, died.

886. Among the deaths published in the California papers we find that Wm. Selleck, of Catskill, died on Aug 12th at San Francisco, aged 30. (Calif. news).

887. A son of Joseph P. Deitz, of Schoharie, about 4, fell into a well and was drowned.

888. Nicholas H. Hallenbeck, 74, father of Jacob Hallenbeck of Guilderland, Albany County, was burned to death in a house fire on the 5th inst.

October 5, 1850
889. Sunday last, in this village, William L. Russell, aged 39.

890. Sep 25, Kingston, John L. Eckert, aged 39 years and 6 months.

891. Sep 28, Kingston, Anna, child of Christian F. and Rosina Philips, aged 15 months and 28 days.

892. Sep 23, Catskill, of consumption, Harriet C., youngest daughter of Malcom W. Mead, aged 17 years and 3 months.

893. Mr. Thomas Johnson, a printer, who was so badly injured by the accident on the NY and Erie Railroad, died on Wednesday last, leaving a wife and several children.

894. By the death of Col. Wm. Croghan, of Pittsburgh, recently deceased, his daughter, who some years since eloped with Capt. Schinley, of the British Army, comes into the entire possession of an estate valued at 5 millions of dollars. Mrs. Schinley resides at Southampton, England.

895. A man named Butler was shot near Essex in the town of Saybrook, Conn. on Sunday night last.

896. A man named Fagan, employed in the Floor Cloth Factory of the Messrs. Powers of Lansingburgh, died very suddenly on Tuesday night. Cholera was the cause. In the afternoon he attended the funeral of Mrs. A. E. Powers.

897. Jno. Clark, of Calais, Me. was drowned off
the Sophia, of Portland, Me. on the 3d ultimo.

898. Foote and Mc Caffray were both hung for
murder at New Haven, Conn. on Wednesday.

899. Mr. John Wilson of 78 Watts st., NY was
instantly killed in a freak accident in New York
on Saturday last. John Mc Cormick died at the
Hospital from the effects of the same accident.

900. Milton Jones, who murdered, in May of last
year, in Illinois, Joseph Miller, his travelling
companion, has been sentenced to be hanged at Mt.
Carmel, Ill. on the 11th of October.

October 12, 1850
901. Oct 11, in this village, John Rush, aged 40.

902. A young man named Edward Terwilliger was
found dead in one of the canal basins at Honesdale
on Oct 7th.

903. On Thursday week, at Vienna, Capt. Heymons,
of Dorchester county, Md., was stabbed to death by
Thos. Grinnan.

904. A German named Agatha Fauss was killed on the
railroad on Tuesday evening of last week near
Reading, Pa.

905. Mr. Schuyler Elliott, a farmer of Thompson,
Ct., hung himself a few days since.

906. A lad, aged 17 years, named Proverst, was
instantly killed in New Brunswick on Saturday.

907. David L. Lester, 6 and Stephen V. Lester, 8,
brothers, were killed at the home of their uncle
David Lester, in Westerlo, Albany county, by a
young man named Dunbar, step-son of the uncle.

908. In the riots at Sacramento, Sheriff Mc
Kinney, Mr. Woodland, George W. Henshaw and
Madison Kelley were killed.

909. Rev. Mr. Greenbench, of West Chester, NY, was
accidently shot in ascending the Chagres on the
10th ult. (from Panama).

910. Phoeba Sharpless, daughter of Aaron
Sharpless, a teacher near Hamerton, Chester

County, Pa., was shot to death on Saturday morning
before school started.

October 19, 1850
911. Oct 7, town of Kingston, Elizabeth Brown,
wife of James Brown, aged 40.

912. On Saturday night last, at Hartford, the wife
of Deacon Comstock, of Hadlyme, fell into a fit
with a candle in her hand. Her clothes took fire
and she was burned to death.

913. Charles W. Scott, from West Desden, Yates
county, NY, was caught in the machinery at
Perrin's Mill, Marshall, on the 1st inst. and
died. (Detroit Tribune).

914. Hiland Hill, Esq., Cashier of the Catskill
bank, died of apoplexy on the 10th inst.

915. Edward Jordan was drowned while passing on
the Hudson River Railroad on Sunday at Speyten
Duyvel Creek. He had been married 3 months.

916. W. S. Birch, who was convicted in Jan 1848,
died at the Baltimore city jail on Friday from the
effects of chloroform.

917. Hannah S. Wilson, aged 91, died last week in
Boston.

October 26, 1850
918. Rev. Mr. Padden, pastor of the Free Baptist
Church, Fabius, NY, died of malignant dysentery.

919. The Charlottstown (Prince Edward Island)
Gazette announces the death, on the 10th inst. of
His Excellency, Sir Donald Campbell, Lieutenant
Governor of that Province.

920. Thomas Carpenter, proprietor of a public
house at Madison, Va. Court House, was shot dead a
few days ago by a man named Edmund Clore, who
escaped.

921. Manco C. Dickinson, only son of Senator
Dickinson, died at Binghampton on Thursday last,
in his 22nd year.

922. Dr. Bureaud Rioffrey died at San Francisco
early in September.

923. Jenny Lind was 30 years old on the 8th of
October. Barnum will be 41 on the 5th of July
next.

924. Daniel Belknap died at Rockton, Herkimer
County, on the 26th ult. at the advanced age of
86. A school-mate of De Witt Clinton, he took
part in the war of the Revolution.

925. Thursday, Mrs. Henry A. Wise, daughter of
Hon. John Sergeant of Pa., died.

926. Deaths on board the Crescent City on her
voyage to Chagres include: John W. Haskell,
Boston; Dr. E. Cuthbert, Newburn, NC; Samuel
Strickland, Rodman, Jefferson county, NY; and John
Houghton, Windsor, Vt., all under 36 years of age.
(Calif. news).

927. Captain Sanger was killed by Indians at
American Bar, Feather river. He was formerly of
Massachusetts.

928. Edward E. Haviland, of NY, lost his life on
the bay of San Francisco on the 6th of Sept.
Albert H. Clarke, of Pa., survived. (Calif.
news).

929. Major Baldwin, formerly of Baldwinville, died
on Monday morning. (Calif. news).

930. Wm. C. Carman, formerly of NY, died at San
Francisco. (Pacific News, Sep 15).

931. Mr. Wm. H. Anderson, of Schenectady, an
engineer on the Utica and Schenectady railroad,
was killed on Tuesday morning at Palatine Bridge.

932. On Wednesday the body of Patrick Laverty
about 25, a laborer on the railroad above Red Hook
landing, was found floating near the west shore of
the Hudson river opposite this village. He had
last been seen on the 14th inst.

933. General James Hamilton will give a eulogy for
Mr. Calhoun on Mar 31 next, the first anniversary
of his death.

                    November 9, 1850
934. Oct 30, Wawarsing, Levi Ostrander, Esq.,
about 48.

935. Oct 23, Esopus, Thomas Lawrence, in his 80th year, a member of the Society of Friends.

936. Sir Walter Raleigh was beheaded in the old Palace yard at Westminister on the 29th of October, 1618, 230 years ago.

937. The Bangor Mercury has a account of loss of life which occurred at Orono, Me. on Tuesday afternoon the 29th ult. Dead include Joseph Clark of Orono, about 55, leaving a wife and several children; Joseph W. Wilson of Palmyra, leaving a wife and two children in this city; John W. Whiton of Saco, unmarried; and Samuel A. Curtis of Exeter, 24, unmarried.

938. R. W. Singleton, Esq., member elect to the House of Representatives from St. Luke's Parish, SC, died on the 21st instant at Grahamsville.

939. The Zanesville (Ohio) Gazette records the death of Mr. and Mrs. John Grieve on Monday.

940. Hiram Bland is to be hung in Greene Co., Ky., on Friday, Nov 14th for the murder of Wm. Walker.

941. John Thompson, while gathering nuts in the town of Lloyd on Friday afternoon last, fell 10 feet out of a tree and his brains were literally dashed out on the rocks.

942. Franklin West, leaving a wife and 6 children in Georgia, died on the 23rd of September in Vera Cruz. (New Orleans Picayune, 20th).

943. Hon. Samuel Young died at his residence in Ballston Spa on Saturday evening, in his 71st year. (Alb. Argus).

November 16, 1850
944. John A. Butler was cruelly murdered near his residence on the 23rd ult. by two negroes. (Edgefield (SC) Advertiser).

945. W. Gorsuch was killed at Hollidaysburg, Pa. on the 29th ult. at a house of ill fame, by a man named Deary.

946. Three bodies were driven ashore at Montauk Point on Monday. One of them was the body of a man supposed to have been Capt. Ezra Gibbs. The others were not identified.

947. Nov 16, Kingston, Miss Sarah Van Gaasbeek, aged 55.

948. Nov 14, Kingston, Ann Eliza, daughter of George Wells, aged 14.

949. Nov 13, Flatbush, Margaret, wife of Lawrence Osterhoudt, aged 71.

950. Two persons named Mc Lelland, a brother, aged 20 and sister 16, were killed on Thursday evening of last week on the Hartford, New Haven and Springfield Railroad near the old Berlin station when the train hit the wagon they were in.

951. The body of Bruner Nichols, of Clarke County, Ky., was found in a well on Saturday last.

952. The northern stage coach rolled over an embankment and Dr. Flanders, aged 50-60, of Londonberry, NH, died. (St.Johnsbury (Vt.) Caledonian).

953. Richard M. Johnson died at his residence in Scott county, Ky. on the 19th. He was born in 1785. (NY Eve. Post).

954. Nov 25, Kingston, Francis Augusta Shaw, aged 7 years, 3 months and 22 days.

955. James Tyler, Jr., a wool merchant of Boston, blowed his brains out on Cambridge Bridge on the 22nd inst.

956. Hon. John Richardson, aged 35, died at Clifton Springs, Ontario Co., on the 20th inst., leaving a wife and 3 children.

957. In the explosion on Saturday of the propeller Resolute at the bottom of pier No. 13, East River, Wm. Shepard, the engineer, leaving a wife and 3 children, burial in Norwich, Conn.; Samuel F. Hall, cook, colored, about 40, leaving 2 children living on Delancy st.; Woodhull Kemble, a deck hand, died at the City Hospital; Joseph Plummer, a fireman; and Woodhull Hartman, the captain, 32, leaving a wife and 3 children residing in Brooklyn, all died. Thomas Watts is mortally injured. (NY Tribune of Monday).

958. George W. Beck, of Bourbon Co., Ky., was shot
dead at Murderer's Bar, on the American Fork, by
William H. Walker of Evansville. (Calif. news).

959. Levi Olenderf, a hand on board the steamboat
Robert L. Stevens, drowned here on Sunday evening
by falling overboard.

960. On Saturday evening last, Patrick O'Rielly,
40, was found lying in the highway near Penn Yan
with his head horribly battered with a club. He
lived 5 hours.

961. A telegraphic dispatch, dated Berlin, Nov 6,
states that the Duke of Brandenburg, Prime
Minister, died that morning. (Foreign news).

December 7, 1850
962. Nov 16, in this village, Armenia, daughter of
Thomas and Emeline Allard, aged 3 years, 28 days.

December 14, 1850
963. Milton J. Traver, Esq., a member of the
Alabama legislature in 1845 was murdered near
Auburn, Macon county, on the 20th ultimo.

964. Jonathan C. Foster of Beverly, Mass., and
Jas. Guild of Sharon, Mass., died on board the
Georgia and were buried at sea. (Calif. news).

965. Mr. Levi Gilbert, aged 24, of Brooklyn, NY
died Oct 28th leaving a wife and 2 children in
Brooklyn. (Calif. news).

966. Mr. W. Coult and wife were killed above
Concord, NH when the train hit their wagon on Dec
4th.

967. The ship Sacuso, Capt. Grace, from Boston
arrived on the 4th of October and was quarantined
8 days, in consequence of Capt. Howard having died
at sea when 36 days out. (from Buenos Ayers).

968. The trial of Albert Bahan for the murder of
Nathan Adler in the town of Venice, ended at
Auburn, verdict, guilty, to be hung Jan 24th.

December 21, 1850
969. Dec 6, in this village, at the residence of
Wm. S. Burhans, Edward A. Burhans, aged 17.

970. Dec 14, in this town, Doct. Conrad Newkirk, aged 85.

971. Tuesday last, Kingston, Irwin Pardee, aged 64.

972. The headless body of John Francis Henry Portner was found in South Chili, NY. He was 30 and from the canton of Vaud in Switzerland.

973. Bennet Bronson, Esq., died at Waterbury Bank, Conn., on the 12th, aged 75. He was a lieutenant in John Adams' Army raised in 1799.

974. Ex-Governor William Plumer, of NH, died at Effing in that State last week, aged 94.

975. Louis or John Carbonneau, of Montreal, was murdered near Detroit on Tuesday last.

976. Arnold Henckel, formerly Sheriff of Comal co., committed suicide on Nov 25th at New Braunfels. (Calif. news).

977. Reuben Dunbar has been found guilty of the death of Stephen V. Lester.

978. Three hands were drowned in their berths on Friday, Dec 6th in the Rondout, Jacob Vernooy of Port Benjamin, 25; Jacob and Thomas Vanwagenen, brothers, of Alligerville, aged 18 & 15. (Rondout Courier).

979. The names of the persons shot at Rhinebeck during the railroad riots a short time ago were Patrick Mc Ewen and Francis Shearin.

980. William Smith, of Johnston county, NC, was killed by his negress who used an axe.

December 28, 1850
981. James Gallagher was hung at St. Louis on Friday for the murder of Mary Crosby.

982. Maria Kenny, a parasol maker, was recently killed in Brooklyn.

983. On the 3rd ult., Hugh Dixon, a Delaware Indian and Calvin Evarts were killed. (Calif. news).

984. Sister Seraphina, Miss Kate Pendergast, daughter of Charles of that city, died in a nunnery at Baltimore, last week. (Springfield Republican).

985. Edward C. Storm, formerly of this village, and son of A. G. Storm, Esq., was among the victims by the explosion of the boiler of the steamer Anglo Norman, at New Orleans, on the 12th inst. (Poughkeepsie Eagle).

986. Duren Moore and his wife Charity Gove, who was possibly of Living Creek, NC were found murdered on the 6th inst., near Thomas, Georgia.

January 4, 1851
987. Jan 3, in this village, Henry Barclay, Esq., in his 73rd year.

988. Dec 29, in this village, John W. Kearny, Esq., in his 73rd year.

989. Jan 1, Ezra Barber, about 18.

990. Jan 2, William, son of William and Nancy Hannah, aged 3.

991. Ex-Governor Bell, of NH, died at Chelsea on the 23d. (Boston, Dec 28).

992. Curtis Watfield, 55, who resided with his son at Franklin, near the village of Croton, committed suicide on Monday. (Del. Gazette).

993. George Hayward, depot master at Lincoln, Mass., caught a robber breaking into the depot. While chasing the robber, Hayward was killed. (Boston, Dec 28).

994. Ex-Governor Plumer died at Epping, NH on the 23d Dec, aged 92. (Boston, Dec 28).

995. Edward Kent, a youth who was beaten by a gang of rowdies on Christmas day, died this morning. (Baltimore, Dec 27).

996. Daniel Miller, an Englishman engaged in the provision business, hung himself last night at his residence in Kensington. (Philadelphia, Dec 27).

997. Henry Sancey, a German, cut his throat last night in Kensington. Cause jealousy.

(Philadelphia, Dec 27).

998. Killed in an Indian attack on the train of
Lewis & Coons, Nicholas Andleas, a German; Chas.
Pavousky, a Pole; William Brown and Peter Logan,
American. (Western Texan).

999. Mr. Wm. W. Case, aged 25, jumped from the
window of his room at the Howard Hotel in NY on
Saturday.

1000. Philip Cornelius, about 65, a resident of
the north part of the town of Stuyvesant, was
frozen to death on the 18th inst. near the house
of Mr. Levi Shufelt, in this town. (Kinderhook
Sentinel).

1001. The cars that left Columbia, on the 24th, on
the Charlotte Road, had just entered the trestle
at Elkin's Mill when they dropped. Nicholas
Gibson, Depot Agent at Winnsborough and a child of
Mr. and Mrs. Powell died from contusions.

1002. The venerable patriot Mr. Jeremiah Powell,
of Middle Settlement, NY, reached 100 on Sunday
last. He was in the army a long time, took part
in the battle of Saratoga. (Utica Herald).

1003. Capt. French's California Company were
attacked near Carlites, Mexico. Mr. Harvis was
killed and Mr. Shepherdson, formerly from San
Antonio, also died. (San Antonio Western Texan).

1004. Lost in the burning of the steamer South
America on the Mississippi, Mrs. White, wife of
the carpenter; Jackson Noles, chief cook; Wm.
Sheppard, the porter, from Evansville, Ind., and
many others unnamed. (N. O. Picayune).

1005. Judge Hallyburton passed a sentence of death
upon Clements and Reid, the two sailors recently
convicted of piracy and murder on board the schr.
J. B. Lindsay. They will be executed on Jan 31st,
proximo. (Richmond Va. Times, Dec 28).

                    January 18, 1851
1006. Jan 17, Mrs. Catharine Barclay, relict of
the late Henry Barclay, in her 70th year.

1007. Jan 12, in this village, at the residence of
his son-in-law Charles Stewart, Esq., Nathaniel
Chittendon, in his 71st year.

1008. Addison Gilmore, President of the Western Railroad, fell dead in the ball-room at Watertown last night, about 50. (Boston, Jan 11).

1009. John Bolt committed suicide last evening. (Buffalo, Jan 11).

January 25, 1851

1010. Dec 6, Sharon, Conn., Anna S. Woodruff, sister of Mr. James Woodruff, aged 68.

1011. Jan 15, Worcester, Mass., of injuries received on the railroad, Francis Schoonmaker, of this village, aged 28.

1012. Henry Barclay, deceased, was the son of Col. Thomas Barclay, who died in New York in 1830 and the grandson of Henry Barclay, D. D., Rector of Trinity Church, New York, who died there in 1764.

1013. Mrs. Jerusha Frederick died at Bangor, Me., Dec 19th, aged 100 years, 5 months. A widow of a seaman who fought in the memorable battle of the Bonne Homme Richard.

1014. Capt. John A. Patterson and Benj. J. Knapp of New York, died in San Francisco of cholera on Dec 6. (Calif. news).

1015. Mr. W. W. Forsaith, formerly pressman of the Boston Times, died recently. (Calif. news).

1016. Jan 5, Baten Rouge, Thomas Muse was murdered. (N. O. Delta).

1017. Accounts from New Zealand state that John Heki, one of the chiefs formerly engaged in conflict with the British, had died at Karkoai, of pulmonary congestion. (Foreign news).

February 1, 1851

1018. Jan 26, in this town, Lavina Eliza, second daughter of Samuel P. and Maria Freligh, in her 20th year.

1019. Jan 28, in this village, Elizabeth, daughter of Peter and Susan Russell, aged 3 years, 21 days.

1020. Jan 22, Kingston, Mary Ophelia, daughter of Frederick and Harriet Kent, aged 1 year, 10 months and 7 days.

1021. The mayor of Princeton, Dr. Jeremiah Dunn, was killed by being thrown from his sulky on Tuesday night, between Trenton and Princeton.

1022. We learn from the Philadelphia North American that the Rev. Walter Colton, Chaplain of the U. S. Navy, died on Wednesday afternoon.

1023. The papers record the death of Purser Samuel Hambleton of the United States Navy. He died on Saturday at his residence on the eastern shore of Maryland, in his 74th year.

1024. Mr. Fayette Harris, aged 23, while standing in the wheel pit of Williams Tannery, in Gregg, Lewis Co., was killed instantly.

1025. Mr. Silas Brewster, about 45, of the town of Wright, Schoharie Co., was killed in the woods on Monday last.

1026. Albert Bahan, convicted of the murder of Alder, the pedlar, was executed at Auburn on Friday. His brother John claimed the body.

1027. John James Audubon, the ornithologist, died at his residence on the banks of the Hudson, Jan 27, 1851, aged 76 years. He was born in Louisiana. (NY Evening Post).

1028. The Mayor of Buffalo offered a reward of 300 dollars for the apprehension of the person who robbed and killed Mr. Harkner.

1029. A negro named Williams was assaulted brutally by several white persons, at Sadsbury, Lancaster Co., on the night of the 16th and carried off. The alarm was given as soon as possible, and a band of colored people, armed with double barrelled guns, were soon on the ground; but they were a few moments too late.

1030. At Porter Me., William Bickford died when a horse kicked a gun he was holding, causing it to discharge into his breast.

February 8, 1851
1031. Last Sunday, in this village, Peter Post, about 76, one of the oldest citizens of Saugerties.

1032. Thursday, in this village, Caroline, wife of Nicholas Swarthout, aged 27.

1033. On Thursday, as the ship Iowa was passing down the Lower Bay, NY, the second mate John Churchhouse, and a seaman, were drowned.

1034. On the 20th inst., Samuel Page, a young man of Charleston, SC, in attempting to pass from one car to the next, slipped and was killed.

1035. Mrs. Martha Myers, 89, last survivor of the massacre of Wyoming, died at Kingston, Lauzerne county, (Pa.) on the 4th inst. Her father, Thomas Bonnet, was one of the 40 white men who built the stockade called "Ferry fort".

1036. On Saturday, an infant daughter of Mr. Thomas Ward, of South Boston, was burned to death.

1037. Reuben Dunbar was executed today. (Albany Eve. Journal, Jan 31).

February 15, 1851
1038. The wife of Henry Z. Hayner, of Troy, committed suicide on Sunday afternoon, leaving 5 children.

1039. John Kiernan, late of the village of Catskill, was found dead in the bar room of Mr. Briggs Rider, in the town of Hunter, on Monday morning last. (Catskill Whig).

1040. On Feb 2, Jacob Carpenter, of Haverhill, Mass., steerage passenger on the Empire City, was found dead in his berth. (Calif. letter).

1041. A young man named Vickery, who was to have been married at Cleveland, Ohio, on the 18th ult., postponed the wedding two weeks. But he died a few days afterwards.

February 22, 1851
1042. Feb 15, in this village, Alice Augusta, daughter of Stephen and Catharine Webster, aged 1 year, 9 months and 15 days.

1043. Feb 18, in this village, at the residence of J. V. L. Overbagh, Caroline Louisa, daughter of Elijah and Elena Dubois, of Kingston, aged 14 years, 4 months.

1044. Feb 17, in this village, Norman Suydam, son
of Peter and Eliza Roosa, aged 1 year and 6
months.

1045. Feb 18, in this village, Mary Augusta,
daughter of Stephen C. and Augusta Ann Lusk, aged
1 year and 3 months.

1046. Feb 9, Catskill, Wilhelmus Schuneman, Esq.,
in his 85th year.

1047. Clinton Hubbard, 25, editor of the Kane
County Democrat, Ill., was found frozen to death
near St. Charles on the 22nd ult.

1048. Abner Estes and his brother-in-law B. Estes,
died, both leaving a wife and children.
(Frankfort Commonwealth).

1049. When the ice started moving in Albany on
Saturday, Robert Elder and William H. Tysdell, who
were attempting to cross, drowned. (Journal,
Monday).

1050. Mr. Seward, of the firm of Seward, Turck &
Co., of Galveston, was drowned in crossing the
East Fork of the San Jacinto river on Jan 27th.
(from Texas).

1051. Major Devazac died in New York on Saturday
morning.

March 1, 1851
1052. Saturday morning last, in this village, John
Henry Montross, aged 11 years, 5 months and 12
days.

1053. Betsey Mc Donald, 26, leaving 2 children,
and Bridget Convey and Nancy Kearnan were killed
at Hyde Park on Tuesday last, all married. One
was 40, leaving 5 children, the other was 25.

1054. The dwelling of Mrs. Swinden, near Macon,
Ga., was destroyed. She and 4 children died.

1055. The magnificent steamer Autocrat, bound from
New Orleans to Memphis, collided on the 9th inst.,
with the steamer Magnolia. Capt. Grant J.
Ferguson and child and Mr. Goodyear, 3d engineer,
are among the lost.

1056. The packet ship Isaac Webb was twice struck by lightning, John Sutton and Edward Jenkins, seamen, were killed.

1057. James R. Graham was recently arrested at Eaton, Ohio, on a charge of murdering Wm. A. Low, 11 years ago, at the town of Lexington, Ill.

1058. A man and his wife, named Grieve, recently committed suicide at Braintree, Ohio.

March 8, 1851
1059. Feb 6, in this town at the Union Tannery, Ellen, daughter of Eli and Pauline Rightmyer, aged 1 year, 2 months and 11 days.

1060. Feb 16, Syracuse, Mrs. Catharine Carson, formerly of this village, aged 75.

March 15, 1851
1061. Mar 7, in this town, Rev. John Crawford in his 91st year.

1062. Mar 2, in this town, Albert J., son of Andrew J. and Elizabeth Brink, about 8 months.

1063. Mar 10, in this town, Maria, wife of Samuel Weeks.

1064. John Fisher Clayton, son of the Hon. J. M. Clayton, of Delaware, died on Tuesday last at his father's residence.

1065. George Spencer, the builder of the houses in Twenty first street which fell about two months ago, died at his residence in Twenty-fourth street on Monday night.

1066. Lost from the steamer Empire City on Friday Feb 21, L. Viel, from Havre, a coal passer, employed on board.

1067. Died on board the Empire City, Tuesday, Mar 7, Johann Lockner, a German laborer from near Erie, Pa.

1068. Judge Dickenson, formerly judge of the Supreme Court of Arkansas, died recently in Corpus Christi. (Texas items).

1069. Mr. & Mrs. Cosden were killed on the 27th ult., near Georgetown Cross roads, Kent co., Md.

1070. Rev. John Crawford, who died recently,
fought in the Revolutionary war at the battle of
White Plains. Taken prisoner, he spent three
months in the Old Jail in New York. He has been
an itinerant minister of the Methodist Church for
37 years.

March 22, 1851
1071. Mar 18, in this village, Francis Edward, son
of John and Sarah M. Field, in his 4th year.

1072. Capt. Sheldon Thompson, an old resident of
Buffalo, died on the 13th inst.

1073. Three laborers on the Grand Junction
railroad, near Boston, were killed on Tuesday,
Patrick Calegan, Richard Barry and Jeremiah
Sullivan.

1074. Henry Gridley, of Oneida Depot, Madison Co.,
committed suicide on Sunday last, leaving a wife
and 5 children. He was Presbyterian.

1075. Hon. Francis T. Brooke, formerly
aide-de-camp to General Washington, died near
Fredericksburgh, Va., on the 3rd instant.

1076. A serious affray resulting in the death of
an Irishman named Joseph Langdon, occurred in
Albany on Saturday night.

1077. Milo Prather, of Jackson county, Ind., came
to his death about the 1st inst., from the effects
of falling into a heap of burning logs, while in a
convulsive fit.

1078. We regret to learn by a dispatch from a
friend at Camden, says the Columbia (SC)
Telegraph, that Gen. George Mc Duffie expired at 9
o'clock A. M., March 11, at the residence of
Richard Singleton, in Sumter.

1079. Teachers have left New York for Oregon; Miss
Miller of Argyle, Miss Wands of Albany, Miss Smith
of Lima, NY, Miss Gray of Townsend, Vt. and Miss
Lincoln of Portland Me.

1080. Burroughs, who was convicted of perjury,
died in the State Prison on Saturday, of brain
fever.

March 29, 1851

1081. John S. Skinner, Esq., about 70, editor of
the Plow, Loom and Anvil, a monthly magazine of
Philadelphia, died at Baltimore on Friday.

1082. Mr. Brooks, formerly of Dey street and
Broadway, New York, was killed in the massacre on
the Isthmus of the Chagras River in Panama.
(Calif. news).

1083. Hon. Isaac Hill, about 70, of New Hampshire,
died at Washington city on Saturday. His native
place is Charlestown, Mass.

1084. Major Mordecai M. Noah died on Saturday last
in New York city. He was born in Philadelphia on
July 19, 1785. Married in 1827, he leaves an
afflicted wife and several children.

1085. Abraham Clearwater was killed by his father
John Clearwater on Sunday night. Kitty
Clearwater, wife of Jeremiah, also a son of John,
was also imprisoned. (Ulster Rep.).

1086. Three children of Mr. Phillips, of
Woonsocket, were lost in a house fire. (Worcester
Tribune).

April 5, 1851

1087. Mar 29, Kingston, Mary Ann, wife of Geo.
Elmendorf, aged 33 years, 5 months and 10 days.

1088. Mar 20, Olive, Plint Barton, about 55.

1089. George Nesbitt, 22, and Robert Nesbitt, 18,
brothers, and Michael White were killed in an
explosion of Fire damp in Washington Company's
coal mine at Fort Griffith, Pa.

1090. Mr. Walter Edelin, of Prince George's
County, Maryland, was shot on Tuesday.

1091. Col. Allen Spencer, of New Lebanon, NY, was
accidently killed by a shot from a rifle in the
hands of his only son on Tuesday last.

1092. George A. Chapman, one of the original
proprietors of the Indianapolis State Sentinel,
died on the 15th ult., in his 46th year, a native
of Maine.

1093. Mr. Tate shot Miss Sheperd when she refused
to elope with him, near Lexington, Holmes Co.,
Miss.

April 12, 1851
1094. Apr 9, Kingston, Maria Heermance, about 62.

1095. Apr 2, Flatbush, Abram Whitaker, a soldier
in the Revolution, in his 92nd year.

1096. William Nichols, of Westhersfield, died on
the 13th ult. aged 94 years. He was a native of
Holden, Mass. and fought in the principal battles
of the Revolution.

1097. A German, named Jacob Nebard, committed
suicide in Newark, NJ, on Friday last.

1098. Mr. A. Strong, living near Warrington,
Warren county, was murdered by a negro on the 17th
instant, by a blow from an axe.

1099. Hon. Orville Hungerford, formerly Member of
Congress from Jefferson Co., died at Watertown on
Sunday, aged 61.

1100. Philo N. Rust, of Syracuse, died in New York
city on Thursday of asthma, buried in Syracuse.

1101. Mr. Christopher Jaycox, about 60, was killed
on the Hudson River Railroad 3 miles south of this
village on the afternoon of Thursday last.
(Poughkeepsie American).

1102. Parker French, notorious swindler, was shot
or hanged for highway robbery on the road between
Mazatlan and Durango, according to a letter dated
February 15th from Mazatlan.

1103. The body of Albert Van Etten was found at
Cameron Corners, Steuben county, on the 17th ult.

April 19, 1851
1104. Apr 12, in the city of New York, of typhus
fever, Dr. Samuel P. Whitaker, 31, formerly of
this place.

1105. Mar 12, at the same place, Lewis Peter, son
of the late S. P. Whitaker, aged 1.

1106. Apr 17, in this village, John F., son of
John E. and Elizabeth T. Fenwick, 6 months old.

1107. Commodore Alexander S. Wadsworth, of the
Navy, breathed his last in Washington on
Saturday.

1108. John Frederick, a German, murdered John
Morrison at a Coffee house at San Antonia on the
10th ult.

1109. Miller Hunter, of Searsburgh, was found dead
in a state room of the Barge Minisink, having
committed suicide by taking laudanum. He leaves a
wife and children. (Newburgh Gazette).

1110. Timothy Donovan, or Donavan, from Boston,
was murdered at New Orleans by a man named Clark,
on the 2d.

1111. Mrs. Catharine Carson died in Syracuse on
Feb 16. Interred at Saugerties. This is the first
occasion which "The Metallic Burial Case" has been
used in this village.

1112. Messrs. Middleton and Singleton, belonging
to the US Surveying Expedition have drowned.

April 26, 1851
1113. Apr 16, Samsonville, of typhus fever, Andrew
J. Brink, a resident of Unionville, aged 22.

1114. Apr 15, Kingston, John Demeyer, aged 79
years, 5 months and 6 days.

1115. Apr 4, Ellenville, Henry Roosa, aged 29.

1116. Apr 16, Shawangunk, of congestion of the
brain, Maria Bruyn, relict of Charles Bruyn, and
daughter of the late James Hasbrouck of Kingston,
aged 58.

1117. Theodore Lockie lost his life by the falling
of a steeple during a fearful gale on Monday night
in Boston.

1118. Chas. Russell committed suicide in New
Orleans yesterday. (New Orleans Bulletin, 1st
inst.).

1119. Dr. Charles Kincaid, a native of Scotland, was drowned on the 26th of March while on a fishing excursion to the Colorado. (Texas news).

May 3, 1851
1120. Apr 23, Kingston, Henry Ackerly, about 65.

1121. Apr 27, Kingston, Maria Louisa, wife of Daniel Young, aged 28 years, 6 months and 13 days.

1122. Apr 22, Rondout, of consumption, George A. Mills, aged 36.

1123. Apr 22, Rondout, of strangulated hernia, James Diamond, aged 60.

1124. Mrs. George, of Pa., was killed in a church in Danville, Pa. which was struck by lightning.

May 10, 1851
1125. Apr 29, in this village, Robert Miller, son of Robert and Jemima Coon, aged 5 years, 5 months and 6 days.

1126. May 1, Kingston, Charles, son of William H. and Asenath Aikin, aged 11 months and 15 days.

1127. May 1, Kingston, Catharine, wife of A. G. Low, about 26.

1128. May 6, Wilbur, John Booth, in his 70th year.

1129. On Thursday after the 27th ult., Glasco, Jairus B. Rider of Glasco.

1130. Friday of last week, Kinderhook, Lucas Hoes, Esq., about 65.

1131. On the Mississippi, about 100 miles above Vicksburgh, on the 2d instant, the steamer Webster was burned. Killed, drowned and missing include, Capt. Samuel Reno and wife; Mr. Henry Harrison and child; Mrs. Buckman, wife of the pilot and child; George Bliss, chief Clerk; John Campbell, second do; a child of Mr. Robwin, of New Orleans; Mary Bucknor, colored chambermaid; Henry, the barkeeper, from Cincinnati; J. Mc Carty, Lynchburgh; and a girl belonging to Mc Carty.

1132. John R. Griffith, 16, hung himself in Marple township, Delaware county, on the 17th inst.

1133. On Thursday of last week the sloop Meridian, belonging to Messrs. Goodwin & Van Buren, of Castleton, was struck by a squall near Catskill and capsized. Dead include a deck hand, Rufus Featherly, Mrs. Goodwin, also a Miss Vosburgh.

1134. Christopher Denton died on Saturday near Hornellsville as a result of a railroad accident.

1135. Our community is much excited by reports of the horrible murder of a Mr. Pease, late of Pottsdam, in this county, about 70. A son lives at Kemptville, C. W., and a married daughter in Vermont. (St. Lawrence Republican).

1136. The Fond du Lac Journal related the following: On the 20th of August 1847, Mrs. Phelps, wife of our informant, Abner P. Phelps, died and was buried at Oak Grove in Dodge county.

1137. Our community was, on Saturday morning, says the Philadelphia Ledger, horrified with the report that a diabolical murder had been perpetrated in Roxborough township. Victims were a German named Valentine Bartle, his wife Catharine and an infant about one year old. Three other children survive.

1138. The Rochester Daily Advertiser learns that on Wednesday a Miss M. Lyon, 18, residing in Churchville, was shot by a young fellow, aged 15 years, by the name of Potter.

May 17, 1851
1139. May 13, Kingston, Aghtie, wife of John Tremper, aged 57 years, 10 months.

1140. May 5, Kingston, of consumption, George Thompson, son of David N. and Margaret Thompson, aged 12 years, 11 months and 25 days.

1141. May 11, town of Kingston, George, son of Charles Plough, aged 18 months.

1142. Mrs. D. Hays, only sister of the late President Polk, died in Columbia, Tenn., on Friday week.

1143. Matthew Carragan, who shot David Romer near Belfast, Allegany county, on the 4th of Feb last, will be hung on Jun 20th at Angelica.

1144. J. Warren, formerly of Newburyport, was killed on Wednesday morning, in a railroad accident on the Fitchburgh Railroad.

1145. At Columbus, Ohio, Thomas Spencer has been committed for shooting George Parcels, bar-keeper, at the Franklin House on Sunday week.

1146. Andrew Egbert, about 45, of Veteran, Cheumng county, hung himself on the 3d instant.

1147. On the 27th ult., Macomb, St. Lawrence county, a fire took the life of Sarah Abigail, about 16 months old, only child of Mr. Elkanah L. Patridge.

1148. David Ross, a merchant, was murdered in Milwaukee on the evening of the 4th inst.

1149. Mr. Hiram Dakin, one of the Superintendents of the Poor, died suddenly on Saturday at his residence in New Paltz.

1150. Joseph Knox Boyd, recently deceased in Washington, was one of the volunteers who burned the frigate Philadelphia in the harbor of Tripoli, to prevent the Turks from enjoying their prize.

1151. Patrick Dunnivan, aged 19, died while removing sand from a hill, only son of a widowed mother. (Coxsackie Union).

1152. Kennebunkport, Maine, dated May 7th, Mr. William Tinum committed suicide last evening leaving 6 children. The coroner, Mr. Aoial Kelley, Jr., died while performing the inquest. He leaves a wife and 3 children.

1153. Thomas Green, of Schodack Landing, was killed on the 12th instant by being hit with a rock thrown from a blast.

1154. Joseph M. Wesland was killed when persons maliciously obstructed the track of the Cleveland and Pittsburgh railroad.

May 24, 1851

1155. May 6, in this town, Mr. Herman Dederick, in
his 88th year.

1156. Apr 29, in this village, Robert William, son
of Robert and Jemima Coon, aged 5 years, 5 months
and 6 days.

1157. May 14, Hurley, of consumption, Eliza, wife
of John P. Elmendorf, about 66.

1158. May 17, drowned in the Esopus Creek, John
Woodruff, about 12, son of Elias Woodruff, and
John Thomas Miller, 13, son of the late Franklin
Miller, and grandson of Mr. Frederick Krows.

1159. Near Verona, Mrs. Douglass, wife of the
station-keeper, discovered her child on the track.
She sprang to its rescue and just as she cleared
the track, the engine caught her dress, pulling
her back and killing her instantly. (Utica Daily
Observer).

1160. Miss M. Lyon is likely to recover.

May 31, 1851

1161. May 26, Coxsackie, Frederic W. Myer,
formerly of this village, son of Abm. Myer,
deceased, aged 30 years, 11 months and 18 days.
Burial in Kingston.

1162. May 18, Kingston, Armenia, wife of W. H.
Buckley, in her 28th year.

1163. It is reported that the King of Naples has
died of dropsy. (European news).

1164. Friday, near Croton station, Harriet
Williams, about 40, threw herself on the track of
the railroad, thereby committing suicide.

June 7, 1851

1165. Died at Albany on the 30th ult., Joel
Barlow, about 4, son of Joel T. and Jane Persons,
formerly of this village.

1166. May 13, Shandaken, Maria Davis, wife of
Thos. F. Davis, aged 52.

1167. May 20, Rondout, George Francis, son of the
late Jno. Andrew Wolfer and Catharine Von Beck,
about 5.

1168. Monday, Mr. Frederick W. Myer, of the firm of Lasher and Myer, in his 31st year, leaving a wife. (Coxsackie Union, 28th ult.).

June 14, 1851
1169. Jun 2, Lackawack, of hasty consumption, Mary Amelia, only daughter of James Benedict, aged 17.

1170. Jun 5, in New York at the residence of her son, Mrs. Maria Hoes, in her 65th year, mother of the Pastor of the R. D. Church of Kingston.

1171. Monday last, 24th street near Tenth avenue, New York, Mrs. Hoes, mother of Peter S. Hoes and Rev. J. C. F. Hoes, was killed by a mad ox. She died on Friday. (Herald, 9th).

1172. The trial of Elisha Smith for the murder of Jas. J. Nannery in Rockland, July 1849, was held. Verdict guilty. (Sullivan County Whig).

1173. The trial of Stephen C. Carey, indicted for the murder of George Haywood, Depot Master at Lincoln, on the 27th of Dec last was held. Verdict guilty.

1174. Sunday, Albany, Mr. William H. Cox, of St. Louis, committed suicide. (Albany Eve. Journal).

June 21, 1851
1175. Flatbush, L. I., Jane Catharine Brainerd, infant daughter of L. C. and Catharine H. Miner, formerly of this place, aged 7 months, 10 days.

1176. Jun 15, Kingston, of consumption, Philip Newkirk, aged 66.

1177. Jun 6, Burlingham, Harriet, wife of James Mc Elhone, and daughter of Shubael and Sarah Otis of Shawangunk, in her 34th year.

1178. This morning, in this city, Mr. Jas. Dawes died. He was the owner of a pyrotechnical establishment which exploded. (Jersey City Sentinel, Jun 14).

1179. During the San Francisco fire of May 3, Edward Cahill, brother of Thomas Cahill, is undoubtedly burned to death. (San Fran. Herald).

1180. James B. Weed, only son of the senior editor of the Evening Journal, has died. (Albany Argus).

1181. James P. Johnston, in jail at Milwaukee, committed suicide on May 26th, a native of Delaware county, NY, aged 32.

1182. A. M. Freeman, of Gilead, Maine, shot his wife on Wednesday of last week, then cut his throat. She still lives, but is not expected to recover.

1183. Diamond, who killed his master Tilghman Hunt, was hung at Fayetteville, NC on Friday last.

1184. A horrible murder in Busry, Province of Hainaut, Belgium by Count and Countess Bocarme upon Gustave Fougnies, brother of the countess.

July 5, 1851
1185. Jun 28, Clovesville, Delaware Co., Charlotte A., wife of W. H. Simmons, and daughter of H. W. France, formerly of this village.

1186. John Tilghman, of Newburn, NC, was hung on the 14th ult., for the murder of Joseph J. Tilghman.

1187. In Pelham, NH, Mrs. Moreland was shot and fatally wounded while struggling with her son, aged 16, who had taken his fowling piece to go a gunning, which his mother forbid until he had drawn her some water.

1188. Miss Martha Hibbard, of North Hadley, Mass., aged 20, died while singing at the Orthodox Church.

1189. Judge Turley, of Memphis, Tenn., a few days since, was leaning upon a small cane which shivered with his weight. A splinter penetrated his side resulting in his death.

1190. Honora Mahony, 28, the mother of 4 children was beat to death at Boston on the 29th ult. by her husband, Daniel Mahony.

1191. Thomas Gregory, about 27, of Andes, in this county, was hunting on the 15th ult., with a pistol, which accidently shot, the charge entering near the heart. He was unmarried.

July 12, 1851
1192. Hon. Spencer Jarnagin, formerly U. S.
senator from the state of Tennessee, died of
cholera at Memphis, on the 24th ult., about 56.

1193. Alexander Mc Kinsey, U. S. Consul at St.
Catherines, died on board the ship Banshee, on the
31st of May, on the passage from Rio Janeiro to
Baltimore.

1194. Four horse thieves, named Henry Jenkins,
from Snyder, Frank Houston, Joseph Sloan and
Cleveland were to have been executed in El Dorado
county on the 27th of May. (from Calif.).

1195. Friday, Albany, Hon. William Horace Brown,
Senator from the first district. A native of
Bermont, resident of Queens, in this State.

1196. John Deacon, ship carpenter, 70, fell from
the staging to the floor while working on the US
steamer Fulton in the Brooklyn navy yard on
Thursday and was killed. The deceased was on
board the Enterprise during her engagement with
the Boxer, in the last war with England.
(Springfield Post).

1197. Signor Evangelista, chancellor of the Holy
consulta, was assassinated at Rome, on the 15th of
last month.

July 19, 1851
1198. Jul 12, Catskill, drowned in the Hudson
River, William West, Printer for the Catskill
Recorder and Democrat, aged 33.

1199. Catharine Brady was killed in falling
through a trap door at the Book bindery of Jacob
Brumstead, in New York on the 14th.

1200. A negro named Ransom killed his wife in the
southern part of Spencer, near the Charlton line,
on Friday night. (Worcester Transcript).

1201. Andrew Dana, Esq. died at Wilksbarre, on the
24th ult., aged 85 years. He was a boy at the
time of the ever memorable massacre of Wyoming.
His father and brother-in-law were killed there,
when he fled with his mother, her family and
others to Connecticut.

1202. Doctor Thomas Hunt and J. W. Frost, editors of the New Orleans Crescent, fought a duel at N. O. on the 19th inst., in which the latter was killed.

1203. On Tuesday the 15th, a boat laden with some 19 Irish laborers going to their work was upset on the Rondout at Wilbur, and one, named Flaherty, was drowned. (Ulster Rep.).

1204. The wife of Mr. Wheeler died at West Elkon, Ohio, on Saturday week.

July 26, 1851
1205. Monday last, Kingston, Mrs. Lucretia Keator, about 36.

1206. Jul 17, Hurley, Rebecca, wife of Hyman Rosa, deceased, about 76.

1207. Jul 16, Ellenville, Casper Besemer, aged 81.

1208. Jul 17, Ellenville, Jane Besemer, wife of the former, aged 80.

1209. Oliver Brown, a soldier of the Revolution, died at Templeton on the 17th inst. The last survivor of those who were engaged in the fight at Concord, Apr 19, 1775. (Boston Atlas).

1210. Mr. Robert Mikler, formerly of Savannah, Ga., was killed by his own gun, while hunting in South Carolina.

1211. Captain John Winson, of Sussex County, Del., murdered his wife from jealousy. He is 60, she was 22.

1212. A young woman, 15-16, daughter of Samuel Chambers, was burnt to death near Johnstown Mount, N. J. on Monday last.

1213. Mr. Demaret was murdered near Hackensack yesterday. (Jersey City Sentinel, 12th inst.).

1214. Edward Palmateer, a hand on the sloop Sharon, of New Hamburgh, and who resided on the opposite bank of the river from this place, lost his life on the 20th inst. (Poughkeepsie American).

98

1215. Four men were drowned in San Pablo bay, on the 28th of May. Dr. Reuben Knox, of St. Louis; John Allen, of Burlington, Vt.; James F. Graham, of North Carolina, nephew of Hon. Wm. Graham, Secretary of the Navy; a Mr. Davis, of Maine; and an Indian boy. (from Calif.).

1216. A Long Island Indian named Frank Brewer was found dead in Montgomery st. on the 2d inst. (from Calif.).

1217. Capt. Irving and 11 of his men were destroyed by Indians. (from Calif.).

1218. Peter Marks, a fireman, died on the steamer New World when the cap blew off the steam chest. (from Calif.).

1219. Seven men were drowned at Park's Bar last week. J. Stull, H. Modesburgh, Charles Cox, Mr. Hodge, Samuel Miller, Jorigan, a Frenchman, and Vincent, also French. (from Calif.).

1220. A Sydney convict, who gave his name as Jenkins, and stole a safe, was arrested, tried, convicted and hung by a number of citizens. (from Calif.).

1221. Mrs. Sarah Meritt, of Marbletown, Ulster Co., was found dead in the cellar of her son's house on the 4th inst.

August 2, 1851
1222. Jul 24, in this village, Solomon Myer, about 43.

1223. Jul 18, Rondout, Charlotte, daughter of Donald Mc Millan, aged 7 years, 6 months and 25 days.

1224. Jul 21, Rondout, John Henry, son of John and Margaret Samuels, aged 9 years, 5 months and 15 days.

1225. Jul 15, St. Louis, Mo., of cholera, Joseph Morris Baldwin, formerly of Kingston, aged 36.

1226. George Cobb, a respectable mechanic of Roxbury, Mass., drowned himself in a hogshead of water in his cellar on the 20th ult. He leaves a wife and child.

1227. S. Aldhonson, a young German, committed suicide in Hoboken.

1228. The daughter of Mr. Schoten was killed by a German servant in his house. (Pal. (Mo.) Whig).

1229. The sloop Rebecca Ford, owned and manned by the Oneida Community, capsized and sunk on Saturday the 26th ult., near Hyde Park, on the North river, while on her way from Kingston to New York city, loaded with limestone. Dead were Mrs. Mary E. Cragin and Miss Eliza Allen.

1230. The sentence of the law was executed upon Matthew Carrigan for the murder of David Romer, on Friday last, in this village. (Angelica Era).

1231. Two men, Henry Douglas and E. T. Benson, convicted of the murder of Asa Havens, 2d mate of the bark Glen, on the 17th of Sep, last, were executed in New York on Friday. James Clements, accomplice, has a stay of execution until Aug 22.

1232. Three sons of Henry Hendrickson, residing near Mill Hook, in the town of Rochester, on the 22d inst. secretly conveyed a gun from their father's house for the purpose of shooting squirrels. William, about 13-14 was killed. (Ulster Democrat).

August 9, 1851

1233. Jul 26, Plattekill, Mary Ann Gerow, aged 62.

1234. Aug 3, Kingston, James C. Tappen, aged 30 years, 7 months.

1235. John Redfearn died in a shooting at Manchester on Saturday morning. (European news).

1236. The execution of Count Hippolyte Visart de Bocarme, by guillotine, took place at Mons, in Belgium, on Friday, Jul 18. (European news).

August 16, 1851

1237. Aug 5, Hopeville, Conn, at the home of her son Henry A. Lathrop, Mrs. J. Greenleaf Lathrop, relic of Septemus Lathrop, in her 66th year.

1238. George Cranse was murdered on Aug 5 at Milton Ferry. (Poughkeepsie Eagle).

1239. Wednesday last, town of Kingston, John German, an Irishman, was crushed to death.

1240. Three hands on the steamboat Trojan, Patrick Duggan, William Fuller and Anthony Mc Nulty, were burned to death on the 7th in New York city, when the boat was destroyed by fire.

August 23, 1851
1241. Aug 17, of consumption, Eliza, wife of William Beatty, aged 53.

1242. Aug 13, Kingston, Rodney Baldwin Clay, aged 9 months, 24 days.

1243. Aug 15, Kingston, Annah, daughter of Jacob and Helenah C. Plough, aged 9 months, 4 days.

1244. Aug 14, Rondout, Nathan J. Beebe, in his 55th year.

1245. Aug 17, Plattekill, Mrs. Joanna Van Steenbergh, aged 60.

1246. Jerry Blake, a clerk in the store of E. Clausen, of Utica, was drowned this afternoon, leaving a wife.

1247. C. H. Gherkin, professor of music, ordered his coffin on Saturday last, and died that evening.

1248. On Sunday last a fight broke out between a white man named Snyder and George, a negro, belonging to the estate of Henry Bevans, deceased. Both were drowned. (Cumberland Civilian).

1249. James Donohue, a deck-hand on the steamboat R. L. Stevens, was lost overboard near Poughkeepsie on Tuesday evening last.

August 30, 1851
1250. Aug 6, in this village, Frederick Smith, son of William and Catharine Krows, in his 7th year.

1251. Ex-Gov. James Mc Dowell, of Virginia, died on Saturday at his residence near Lexington.

1252. The five sons of Mr. Onacker died in a house fire at Brighton, five miles from Cleveland.

September 6, 1851

1253. The minutes of the meeting of the IOOF of Sep 1 mention the death of the wife of Abram F. Calkins.

September 13, 1851

1254. On Sunday last, at Prince street, New York, Mrs. Carr, one of her children and a child of a boarder, died from eating a pudding in which arsenic, instead of soda, was used.

1255. Henry Wooden, of Canandaigua, whose wife, about six years ago, was found in a well near his house, has been indicted for killing her.

1256. At Philadelphia, Mm. <sic> Lovett, was bitten by a rattlesnake and died the next day.

1257. We learn from the Ellenville Journal that Mr. George P. Downs of Sandburgh died in an accident on the 2d inst. (Ulster Rep.).

1258. Robert E. Bradshrw, <sic> from Mass., about 22 and William A. Simpson, from Charleston Mass., about 24, miners, were murdered Aug 13, in the Chilian Gulch. (Latest Calif. news).

September 20, 1851

1259. Sep 9, in this village, Mrs. Dorcas Schoonmaker, aged 51 years, 6 months.

1260. Wilbur, Laura Emma, daughter of Isaac and Hannah Lenike, aged 1 year, 7 months and 13 days.

1261. Sep 6, Ellenville, Lewis Weller, aged 26.

1262. James Clements, convicted of murder on the bark Glenn, has been pardoned by President Fillmore.

1263. A young man named Cole, formerly of Cairo, Greene County, in the employ of Whiting Weeks, of Kingston, was drowned in the Esopus on Wednesday of last week.

1264. Mrs. Crittenden, wife of Attorney Gen. Crittenden, died Sep 8th at Frankfort.

September 27, 1851

1265. Sep 25, in this village, Ann J., wife of Wm. M. Brink, aged 38, funeral from Reformed Dutch Church.

1266. The evening of the 22d was very dark, and about 9 o'clock Abraham Levi, about 24, a German Jew peddler, walked off the dock at the foot of Canal street, Rondout, and was drowned. (Ulster Rep.).

1267. Taylor Murphy was found guilty of the murder of his wife and sentenced to be hung on the 10th of Oct, by the Circuit Court of Ky.

1268. Sylvester Graham, founder of the Grahamites, died on Thursday last in Northampton, Mass.

1269. Hon. Frederick Whittlesey died of typhus fever in Rochester, on Thursday of last week. He sat on the Bench of the Court of Appeals in NY.

October 11, 1851
1270. Oct 8, Saugerties, Mrs. Richards, a widow, who leaves several small children.

1271. Captain Warman, of the schooner Walhalla, has apparently drowned on the 1st, opposite Wilbur. (Rondout Courier).

1272. Two sons of Mr. Samuel Clark, of Frantzdale, burned or were suffocated in a boat on the canal on Thursday of last week. (Ellenville Journal).

1273. Mr. Richard C. Vankirk of Ellenville, formerly of NJ, was drowned in Yankee Pond on Friday of last week. (Ellenville Journal).

October 18, 1851
1274. Monday last, Shaler's Tannery, Mr. Daniel S. Quick, of Plattekill Clove, aged 58.

October 25, 1851
1275. Oct 16, Saugerties, Malissa Ann, daughter of Isaac and Sarah Layman, 1 year, 11 months and 9 days old.

1276. Oct 19, Saugerties, Charles Edmond, son of Peter and Ann Layman, 2 years, 3 months and 1 day old.

1277. Margaret Garrity has been acquited of the murder of her seducer Edward Drum, in Newark.

1278. A son of Thomas W. Cornell, about 12, drowned on Saturday last, in the locks at Eddyville.

November 1, 1851

1279. The Rev. Robert Mc Nabb, of Carthage, Moore co., NC, was murdered on Friday night last. (Fay. NC Observer).

1280. The trial of Almira Bezly, for the murder of a child, her half-brother, has been held in Providence, R. I. She was acquited due to insanity.

1281. Mr. Fairbanks, the track superintendent, was killed near Castleton, Rensselaer County, on Friday last.

1282. Pardon Peckham, 92, a soldier of the Revolution, was killed on the rail road track near Buffalo, on the 16th inst.

1283. Three men, including Dr. Sheldon, were killed on the N. Y. and New Haven Railroad, 2 and 1/2 miles from New Rochelle.

November 8, 1851

1284. Oct 31, Coxsackie, Catharine M. Bunchardt, wife of John M. Burchardt, and daughter of Rev. Dr. Woodward, of Middle Haddam, Conn., in her 22nd year.

1285. Oct 24, Poughkeepsie, Mrs. Emily H., wife of George N. Van Deusen, of Kingston, aged 18 years, 3 months.

1286. Oct 25, Kingston, Dr. Andrew Russell, 49 years old.

1287. This morning, Patrick Mc Cluskey was found dead in his bed in North Providence. His wife Alice has been commited for examination. (Providence, Oct 3).

1288. Mrs. Nancy Henfford has been indicted for the murder of Mrs. Samuel Engle, by administering arsenic.

November 15, 1851

1289. On Wednesday, a laboring man by the name of Dewitt, employed at Mr. A. Richards' Planing Mill, in this village, was killed by being revolved around a drum some 300-400 times per minute. (West Troy Advocate).

November 22, 1851

1290. Nov 12, Kingston, Hermania A., daughter of the late J. H. Sutermeister, aged 49 years, 6 months and 29 days.

1291. Last Saturday, at the Rondout dock, John Floughey, a German, about 30, died when a camphene lamp exploded aboard boat 200 of the Penna. Co.

1292. The 2 negroes who killed Mr. Tally, in Louisa county, Va., will be executed on Dec 19th at the Louisa Court House.

1293. An inquest was held on the body of Daniel Mallon, a native of Ireland, about 55, at 599 Greenwich street. He had been killed by a flat iron used by Cecelia Mallon, his wife. (Herald).

November 29, 1851

1294. Nov 23, in this village, at the residence of John Kiersted, Jr., Emma Dickeson, colored, 71 years old.

1295. Nov 22, Kingston, Harvey Keator, about 50.

1296. Nov 18, Rondout, Henry F., in his 5th year, child of Bernard V. K. and Margaret Degroff.

1297. Nov 19, Rondout, Sarah M., in her 3rd year, child of Bernard V. K. and Margaret Degroff.

1298. The Warsaw, New York, tells that Mrs. True, of Dovington, wife of Wm. True, was killed by him, accidently.

1299. A copy of the will of James Fennimore Cooper, proved 26 Sep 1851, names his wife Susan Augusta.

1300. James Duff has been found guilty of the murder of his twin brother in Butler co., Pa.

1301. The Albany Express, on the 25th inst., tells of a tragedy on Monday, on the Delaware Turnpike, 5 miles from that city. John Moore killed his wife, Elizabeth Moore, then himself, leaving 2 children aged 3 and 5.

1302. Samuel Olmstead and Polly, his wife, were indicted for the murder of Olmstead's five year old daughter by a former wife. Wife guilty, husband acquitted. (Illinois State Democrat).

1303. James Montgomery, aged 70, died in England.

1304. Four men, Enoch Brown, Walter Mathews, Robert Seers and Wm. Conquest died in the ruins of Messrs. Hoe's foundry. (Tribune).

December 6, 1851
1305. Dec 5, in this village, Deborah, wife of Frederick Krows, about 71, funeral from Reformed Dutch Church.

1306. Nov 28, in this village, Elizabeth, daughter of Samuel F. and Catharine Wolven, 9 years, 3 months old.

1307. Nov 30, in this village, Charles L., son of Jacob F. and Elizabeth Fullmer, aged 6 years, 4 months.

1308. Nov 2, in this village, Catharine, wife of John Mc Carthy.

1309. Nov 16, Cincinnati, Ohio, Jane Ann Butler, wife of Thomas C. Butler, Jr., formerly of Dashville, in this county, in her 56th year.

1310. Nov 24, Shokan, Jane, wife of Andrew Hill, aged 35.

1311. Nov 29, Hackensack, NJ, of consumption, Rev. Christian Z. Paulison, pastor of the R. D. Church of Glen, Montgomery county, formerly of Marbletown.

1312. Aug 3, Lysander, Onondaga County, Permelia A. Adams, in her 19th year.

1313. Oct 3, Lysander, Onondaga County, John Q. Adams, in his 17th year.

1314. Nov 1, Lysander, Onondaga County, Chalora J. Adams, in his 17th year.

1315. Sep 15, Lysander, Onondaga County, Phebe Ann Adams, in her 21st year.

December 13, 1851
1316. Dec 5, in this village, Miss Amelia Leggett, 26, burial in Berne, Albany County.

1317. Dec 9, in this village, of consumption, David Kearney, son of the late John Kearney, Esq.,

33 years old.

1318. Mr. Moody, of Monmouth, Ct., died recently.

1319. Alexander Lee, one of the most admired song writers of the day, died recently in London.

December 20, 1851
1320. Dec 7, Kingston, Miss Lany Ann Lockwood, aged 32.

1321. Dec 8, Rondout, Gertrude, wife of George Thompson, aged 32.

1322. Dec 12, New York, of billious fever, John Krom, from the town of Olive, aged 22.

1323. Oct 19, San Francisco, Calif., Dewitt C., son of the late John Demyer, aged 26, formerly of the town of Kingston.

1324. An insane man, named Carrigan, living seven miles from St. John, N. B., murdered his wife, two children and an aunt.

1325. Rev. Mr. Bussey was struck by lightning in the Methodist Church at New London, Chester Co., on Sunday last. (Phil. Penn.).

1326. The Washington (In.) Journal says that Thomson Perkins was found frozen on Wednesday.

December 27, 1851
1327. On the 19th inst., the anniversary of the execution of Robert Blum, in Vienna, placards appeared stating, "Robert Blum lives!"

1328. On Saturday morning, a German named Christian Wanner was murdered in Buffalo by his own brother.

1329. The Coxsackie Union of the 24th announces the death of Ambrose Baker, who died on Monday morning last, aged 45.

January 3, 1852
1330. Dec 30, Brooklyn, NY, Theodore Barrel, youngest child of Isaac and Abby C. Winslow, and grandson of the late Theodore Barrell of this place, aged 3 years and 10 months.

1331. Dec 17, in this village, Miss Phoebe Langley, wife of Benjamin Langley, in her 23rd year. She emigrated from England within the past year.

1332. On Friday of last week, in the upper part of our village, a woman named Nosley set fire to her dress. She died the next morning, leaving a husband and 3 children. (Rockland County Messenger).

1333. Madame Sieber 101 and M. Antoine Galland de la Tour, 98, both died recently in Paris, France.

1334. Mrs. Cesilia Mallon was found guilty of manslaughter and sentenced to 60 days in the city prison for killing her husband.

January 10, 1852
1335. Jan 3, Kingston, Magdelena Schoonmaker, 80.

1336. Kingston, Maria, wife of William Thompson, aged 53.

1337. Dec 23, Williamsburgh, L. I., the Rev. Isaiah Waters, in his 79th year.

1338. Adam A. Ramsay, associate editor of the Albany Knickerbocker, died on the 3d inst. at Jacksonville, Florida.

1339. John H. Baldwin, brother of James W. Baldwin, of this village, died on Dec 19th in St. Louis, in his 61st year. (Republican).

1340. Martin Brophy was injured in a fight on Christmas morning, near Mrs. Fiero's tavern, and died a few days later. Justice Fiero held the inquest. Martin Brophy came to his death by blows inflicted by Catharine Conoly, John Farrell, James Noon, William Noon, Luke Cavery, Patrick Winne and Mary Cavony, near the house of Mary Fiero.

January 17, 1852
1341. Jan 3, Cobleskill, at the residence of Nicholas Russell, Sarah Barnard, aged 20, of consumption.

1342. Jan 4, Cobleskill, at the residence of Nicholas Russell, of consumption, Nancy M., wife of Henry S. Russell, aged 36 years, 11 months.

1343. Jan 11, Wilbur, Hubert Smith, 28 years old.

1344. Jan 7, Marbletown, of consumption, James Wood, aged 59 years, 7 months and 14 days.

1345. Jan 2, Rosendale, Jacob A. Snyder, Esq., aged 66 years, 5 months.

1346. Dec 10, Ouachita, La., Hon. George W. Copley, in his 37th year, formerly of Delaware County.

1347. On the 19th of Sept. last, at San Juan del Sud, Mr. Isaac Jerome, of Syracuse, nephew of Judge H. K. Jerome, of Rochester, was most wantonly murdered. (NY Express).

1348. A family of four persons, Philip Brady, his wife, both aged 30, a son, aged 3 and his brother John, aged 18, were suffocated.

1349. Bill Marshall and Judan Verdugo were tried, convicted, sentenced and executed on a charge of having prevailed upon the Indians to murder a man named Slack and 3 others. (from Calif.).

1350. Ellen Sullivan committed suicide on Sunday last. (Po'keepsie American).

1351. Last evening, at Wilbur, George Plass stabbed Abram France, who subsequently died. (Ulster Republican).

1352. Elenor Ann Porden, born in 1795, is the wife of Sir John Franklin, who is missing at sea in the North.

1353. We hear of the death of Mr. John W. Wilson, who died yesterday in this city. (St. Louis Rep., 27th).

January 24, 1852

1354. The widow of J. Fennimore Cooper died suddenly, at Cooperstown, on Monday last, of asthma.

1355. A man named Goble died at Knightstown, Ind. some time since.

1356. A child of John and Bridget Reddy died of injuries received from its father. Inquest held on Wednesday. (Tribune).

1357. A young man named Finch met a sudden death near Ellenville, aged 26, family resides in Catskill. (Ulster Republican).

1358. On the 17th inst., in the District of Richmond, Philadelphia, Arthur Mc Bride, 23, was killed by his brother Andrew Mc Bride, 27.

1359. A negro man named Reuben died, very suddenly, at Northport, L. I.

1360. Capt. Mc Nulty was lost in the explosion of the steamboat Magnolia, near St. Simon's island, on the Mississippi, on the 9th inst.

1361. Archibald M. C. Smith, agent of the Hartford Insurance Company, died when walls of a burning building fell outward in Buffalo on Sunday. Mr. Bean, who was sitting up with the corpse of his child, also died in the fire. (Com. Adv.).

January 31, 1852
1362. Jan 23, in this village, Christopher, son of Francis and Anna Maria Haber, aged 1 year, 9 months and 3 days.

1363. Jan 28, in this town, Peter B., son of Christopher Fiero, Esq., about 18.

1364. Jan 24, Kingston, Catharine, wife of James Kent, aged 41 years, 29 days.

1365. Jan 24, Kingston, of consumption, Elizabeth Arnold, wife of Dr. J. K. Bogardus, aged 25.

1366. Jan 24, Kingston, of consumption, Sarah, wife of Gilbert M. Gillett, aged 45.

1367. Herman Downs Gould died at his residence, in this village, on Monday, in his 53d year. Born in Sharon, Conn., 16 Jun 1799, his uncle Abel Downs, Esq., of Colchester , in this county, died in 1824. In 1825 Col. Gould married the eldest daughter of Samuel Sherwood, Esq., who survives him, and by whom he had 4 sons, the eldest aged 20. A member of the Presbyterian church. (Delaware Gazette).

1368. Dr. A. Sidney Doane, Health Officer of the Port of New York, died yesterday morning at his residence on Staten Island. He was a native of Boston, leaving a wife and several children.

Interrment in Boston. (Tribune).

1369. Miss Miller died on Sunday last in Berke
township, about 7 miles about Reading. (Berke
County Press, 18th).

February 7, 1852
1370. Jan 31, in this village, Theresa Jane,
daughter of Chauncy M. and Catharine Swart, 2
years, 6 months and 2 days old.

1371. Feb 3, Kingston, at the residence of Doct.
J. Myer, Sarah S., eldest daughter of John I.
Gillespy, of Saugerties, 14 years and 4 months
old.

1372. Rev. T. S. Skinner died at Dr. Beecher's
church in Brooklyn, on Friday last. A daughter
survives.

1373. On Monday of this week, near the farm of P.
Elmendorf Cole, Dyer Shepard, of this town, a
member of the Methodist Church, husband and father
of 3, died. (Kingston Journal).

1374. Died at Shipharbor, Dec 29th, Mr. Daniel
Weekes, in his 117th year. Born on Long Island on
3 Dec 1735, served in the British army when the
gallant Wolfe fell, Sep 12, 1758. He adhered to
the royal cause during the revolution, and
received a grant of land at Shipharbor, he brought
up a family of 21 children.

1375. Two executions took place on Friday last,
Knickerbocker, at Buffalo, for the murder of
Harkner, and Lawrence Reiley, at Brooklyn, for the
murder of his wife and mother-in-law.

1376. A Sheffield (Eng.) paper says that the
venerable poet Montgomery has read the notices of
his death.

1377. The body of Jacob Lehman, son of Aaron
Lehman, a German Jew peddler in the District of
Richmond, Philadelphia, was probably found in
Richmond. (Philadelphia Bulletin of Saturday).

February 14, 1852
1378. Feb 7, Kingston, infant child of Jacob
Plough, Jr.

1379. Feb 6, Kingston, William Van Buren, about 35.

1380. John Erpenstein, the German who was convicted for killing his wife in Newark, in December last, will be hung on Tuesday, March 30th.

1381. Thomas Kelly was murdered at Manchester, near Canandaigua, on Saturday night last.

1382. A French professor in the academy of Mr. Churchill, of Sing Sing, named Bordenhave, says the NY Journal of Commerce of the 3rd inst., had been missing since the 1st of January last. His body was found on Tuesday a short distance west of Sing Sing.

1383. Mr. Hiram Wilcox, of Dayton, Ohio, died after being bitten by a drunken loafer.

1384. Mr. G. S. Warren, the returned Californian, who was robbed about 2 weeks since of $400 in cash and his watch and clothes, died last evening. (Phil. Ledger).

1385. Adam Eckfeldt, Esq., who, for nearly half a century, was chief coiner in the US Mint, died in Philadelphia, on the 6th inst.

1386. Chin-chi-ke, captain of the Chicksaw Light Horse, was killed while trying to stop four Seminole Indians returning from Texas with whiskey.

February 21, 1852
1387. Feb 13, in this town, John Harrington, aged 70.

1388. We learn that 3 children of John Fitzpatrick died of scarlet fever, in this town, on the 19th inst.

1389. Ship fever is making fearful havoc in New York; the Captain of the Fifth Ward says: On Saturday last James Brigham, the doorman, died. Yesterday First Assistant Captain Reynolds bid adieu to this world and last night Officer Carlock to his long home.

1390. On Wednesday the mail train stopped at Deposit for dinner, a freight train ran into it

killing a Miss Wisner, from Goshen, Orange, co.,
and an Indian girl.

1391. Mr. Hyatt died in an accident on the New
York and Erie Railroad, on the Delaware river, on
the 17th. (Tribune).

1392. On Monday last, a fatal recontre occurred in
Anderson County between Mr. R. J. R. Baker and Mr.
Woodford Payne. Mr. Payne died. (Shelby (Ky.)
News, 3rd).

February 28, 1852
1393. Feb 22, in this village, of consumption,
Edith, wife of A. Craft, in her 36th year.

1394. Mr. Richard T. Meldron, brother of Mrs.
Peter H. Myer, died in the accident on the
railroad at Deposit. Interred in this village on
Thursday last. <see # 1390>

1395. The Delhi Gazette of the 11th inst. says a
young man of the village, named William Peffer,
died.

March 6, 1852
1396. Feb 28, New York, Fanny, infant daughter of
Joseph Tuckerman, Esq., aged 2.

1397. Mar 2, NYC, Col. Joshua B. Wood, formerly of
Rutland, Mass. and Providence, RI, in his 73rd
year. Father-in-law of Rev. E. A. Nichols, of
this village, Rev. Mr. Bostwick, of Sandy Hill,
and Rev. Mr. Gibson, of West Point.

1398. Feb 13, NYC, Dr. John A. Kiersted, 27,
formerly of this town.

1399. An Irishman named James M'Manus, of Hudson,
employed on the Hudson River Railroad, was
suddenly killed at Stony Point on Wednesday last.

1400. Otto Grunzig, convicted of the murder of his
wife by poison, was executed in New York on the
27th ult.

1401. David Kennison, who had fought in many of
the battles of the Revolution, and is supposed to
be the last survivor of the Boston Tea Party, died
at the residence of William Mack, at Chicago, Feb
24, aged 117.

1402. A man named Steingraver, convicted of murder, was hung at Ashland, Ohio, on the 30th ult.

1403. On Friday, Mr. L. Coe, of Middletown, Conn., was killed while crossing the Hartford and New Haven railroad track at New Britian, 6 miles from Hartford. He was 55, and former sheriff of Middlesex county.

1404. Mr. W. C. Norris, formerly a resident of the city of Albany, was stabbed at San Francisco on the 24th of Jan last. He died the next morning.

1405. Philip S. Hasbrouck, Esq., of New Paltz, conducted an inquest on the body of Francis Valley, who died at the home of Elanor Dubois, in that town. (Ulster Republican).

March 13, 1852
1406. Mar 3, Tivoli, of congestion of the brain, Frances Emma, 2nd daughter of David C. and Marian Nodwell, aged 4 years, 3 months and 13 days.

1407. Feb 21, Brooklyn, of inflammation, Thomas Lamb, aged 27.

1408. On the 5th inst., Jas. White, a shoemaker living in East street, Baltimore, cut the throats of his daughter, 15, and son, 3. He then set fire to the house and cut his own throat. All 3 died.

1409. Sunday morning last, Bloomingburgh, Orange co., at Howard Sease's tavern, a young woman named Levenia Bowen died of appoplexy. (Sullivan County Whig).

1410. The Queen of Madagascar is reported to be dead.

1411. James Mc Bride, who killed his brother while quarrelling at a card table, has been found guilty of murder at Philadelphia.

1412. Dr. Paul T. Taber, son of the Hon. A. Tabor, died at his residence in Missouri, a few days since.

1413. Alexander Levally died on Monday evening, aged 26. (Delhi Express).

1414. Mar 12, Malden, Mrs. Mary Cushing, wife of Rev. Josiah Leonard, in her 31st year.

1415. Mar 14, Plattekill, at the residence of Levi D. Myer, Harvey Myer, in his 25th year.

1416. Mar 2, Tecumseh, Mich., of congestion of the brain, Margaret Lavinia, daughter of Goodrich and Dorcas Baldwin, formerly of this village, in her 8th year.

1417. Capt. George Huggins, a citizen of Mobile, died on the 22d of Feb, a victim of superstitious presentiment.

1418. A gentleman named Williams, about 60, a wealthy mahogony dealer, from Baltimore, was killed on the 16th inst., at Jamesburg, on the Camden and Amboy Railroad.

1419. Seaman, the negro arrested a short time since for the murder of his daughter, was found guilty, at Poughkeepsie. He will be hung on May 7th next.

1420. A man named John Bryon was drowned on the 16th inst. in the Chenango Canal at Clinton.

1421. Henry Jukenberg, a German, aged 50, committed suicide at Philadelphia on March 16th.

1422. Capt. Thomson died when the propeller Gen. Warren was wrecked at the mouth of the Columbia on Jan 31st. 42 others died. (News by the El Dorado).

1423. Thos. J. Crockett, a nephew of the celebrated 'be sure you're right, then go ahead,' David, died at San Augustine in the Redlands, a few days since, aged 40.

March 27, 1852
1424. Mar 20, in this village, Emanuel Roosa, aged 50.

1425. Mar 25, in this village, Marriett, daughter of Francis and Sarah Sudderly, 4 years, 8 months and 7 days old, funeral from the R. D. Church.

1426. Mar 23, Kingston, Mr. Benj. F. Vallet, in his 39th year, a member of Kosciusko IOOF.

(Kingston Journal).

1427. Yesterday morning, near Main street Landing, Abigail Robinson, about 50, was found dead. (Poughkeepsie Eagle of Saturday last).

1428. On Friday night, Detroit, the wife of a man named Bernhoeff was found dead in her house.

1429. In Northampton, Mass., Thursday, Justin E. Bragg, of that town, who rested on the muzzle of his gun when his dog came up and put his paw on the trigger causing instant death.

1430. Within the 5 years since the commencement of the war with Mexico, 13 American Generals have died, viz: Taylor, Worth, Mason, Brady, Kerrney, Hamer, Hopping, Belknap, Duncan, Croghan, Brooks, Arbuckle and Whiting.

1431. Mrs. Ann Hoag was found guilty of murder in Poughkeepsie and will be hung on May 7th next.

1432. W. B. Radcliff was acquitted in the murder of David Ross at Milwaukee.

1433. Died, in this village, on Wednesday the 17th inst., Egbert B. Killey, Esq., about 49. (Poughkeepsie Eagle).

1434. George Nelson, mate of the brig Huntress from New York, was knocked overboard and drowned off Cape Hatteras, on the 10th inst.

1435. Lancaster, Ky., Mar 14, last evening, Russell Hill, Isaiah Hill, John Sellers and William Crisman died in a fight at Scott's Fork of Sugar Creek. (Louisville Courier, Mar 14 & 16).

April 3, 1852
1436. Mar 19, Durham, Greene Co., Mrs. Vina, wife of Edmund Snyder and daughter of James Ransom, formerly of Saugerties, in her 22nd year.

1437. Ex-Gov. Morrow, of Ohio, died at his farm in Warren county, March 22nd, in his 82d year.

1438. Reuben Edmonson, a noted thief, died on the 6th inst., at St. Louis, aged 63.

1439. Hon. J. Holliday, a member of the Indiana Legislature and John Wall, Esq., of the

Mississippi Legislature, have recently died.

1440. A sad affair occurred in a house of ill-fame on the 22d of Feb. A man named Carroll was stabbed by a man named Mc Donald. (from Calif.).

1441. On the 16th ult., Spanish Bar, Mr. Charles H. Dexter and Capt. Daniels were found cut to pieces in their beds. (from Calif.).

1442. Samuel Todd, aged 101 years, 14 days, died in Middletown, Delaware county on the 19th inst., born in New Haven, Conn., funeral at Clovesville, one of the few Revolutionary Fathers left. (Ulster Rep.).

1443. Samuel Preston, editor of the Huron Reflector, in descending his stairs, on the 3d of March, fell and fractured his skull. He died the next morning, in his 74th year.

April 10, 1852
1444. Mrs. Hilt, of Rocky Hill, Philadelphia County, on Tuesday last, murdered her 4 week old child.

1445. Louis de Noyelles, of Haverstraw, was run over by the upward express, near Dobb's Ferry, on Tuesday and instantly killed, leaving a wife and 5 children.

1446. John Bishop, a Revolutionary soldier, died at Rossville, S. C. a few days since, aged 89.

1447. Mr. James Harper, a conductor on the Baltimore and Susquehannah Railroad, fell off the train a day or two since and was killed.

1448. Harvey Kimberly was accidently killed last week in the eastern part of the town of Austerlitz, Columbia county, by W. W. Tosley.

1449. Warren Cobb, of Mansfield, about 60, committed suicide on Saturday evening, leaving a widow and 3 sons.

1450. James Connor died while crossing the railroad track near Jersey City, on Friday.

1451. On Sunday last, Mr. Bookout, of Roxbury, Delaware co., committed suicide by hanging himself.

1452. On Monday, Timothy O'Sullivan fell off the rocks above Captain Field's dock, apparently drowned. Wife lives in New York.

April 17, 1852
1453. Apr 14, in this village, Eugene L., son of Chancy M. and Catharine Swart, aged 6 months, 4 days.

1454. We learn from the Troy Budget, that, as a train was backing up across the bridge at the Greenbush station, a man named Richard Lundy, of that city, was killed.

1455. The late Mrs. Ware, of Frankfort, Ky., has liberated, by her will, all her slaves.

1456. We notice the recent death of Capt. Sir Samuel Brown, the inventor of chain cables, chain bridges and suspension piers.

1457. On Saturday, Edmund Furness, Geo. Bunker, Mr. Burnham and son were drowned near Portsmouth, NH.

1458. Recently, near Huntsville, Texas, from a disease much resembling cholera, a son and 13 negroes of Mr. Calhoun died.

1459. Edmund Glore, convicted of the murder of Thomas Carpenter last fall, was executed at Madison Court-House, Va. on the 26th ult.

1460. Jacob Lentz, an old German, was killed on Friday last on a bridge over the Fallkill, by a train.

1461. Henry Clay's 75th birthday was commemorated on Monday evening.

April 24, 1852
1462. Apr 22, in this village, Emma, wife of Mr. Thomas Welch, in her 28th year, funeral from the R. D. Church.

1463. Apr 22, in this village, John Martin, son of Major and Matilda Egleston, aged 8 months.

1464. Saturday last, Windham Center, George Ellarson, about 50, died at the public house of Ebenezer Belknap, Esq. (Prattsville Advocate).

1465. Apr 14, Ashland, Mr. Milo Wears, about 35. (Prattsville Advocate).

1466. Prince Schwarzenberg died suddenly at Vienna on the 5th inst., from appoplexy, aged 51.

1467. The jury in the case of Maurice Antonia, the Portugeese, convicted of the murder of a man named Pinto, at Rochester, brought in a verdict of guilty. He will be hung on June 3d.

1468. John Donovan, the murderer of James Rowley, at Potsdam, was hung at Canton, St. Lawrence County on the 17th inst.

1469. A five year old daughter of Samuel Springsteel, of Ellenville, a ship carpenter, was burned on the 16th inst. She died a day later.

May 1, 1852
1470. Apr 29, in this town, Mr. Robert L. Brink, aged 69.

1471. Apr 16, Ashland, Mr. Charles Mc Donald, about 60. (Prattsville Advocate).

1472. On Friday last, New York city, Ex-Governor John Young.

1473. Hiram Hixon, about 16, was tried for murder, in November last, of Robert Bush, about 15. Oyer and Terminer Court found him not guilty.

1474. Gen. Solomon Van Rensselaer died at Albany, on the 25th inst., of appoplexy. He entered the army under Wayne in 1782.

1475. The Mother Superior of the Order of the Sisters of Mercy, Josephine Cullen, died at the Convent at Pittsburgh, on Thursday last.

May 8, 1852
1476. Apr 5, Saugerties, Timothy O'Sullivan fell into the Esopus. His body was found on Sunday last.

1477. On the 1st inst., Geo. W. Brotherton, 6, residing in the town of Wilma, Jefferson County, died in an accident in a saw mill. (Watertown Democratic Union).

1478. Prince Paul, of Wurtemberg, died at Paris on the 14th ult. (from Europe).

1479. Marshall Gerard died on the 17th ult. at Paris, in his 79th year. (from Europe).

1480. The wife of Michael Catt, a resident of Decker township, Indiana, was shot recently by her son-in-law, Mr. Young, toward whom she was approaching disguised as an apparition.

1481. Carl Frederick Seeloff, a native of Brandenburgh, Prussia, was killed on the 30th ult. while walking upon the track of the New York and Erie Railroad one mile from Wellsburg.

1482. S. B. Crane, from Peppersville, Mass., committed suicide on the 4th at Bixby's Hotel, NY. A brother John H. Crane of Milleville, Mass., survives.

May 15, 1852
1483. Brownsville, dates to the 28th ult., state that the inhabitants of Rio Grande City were excited by the murder of Mr. Patton by some Mexicans.

1484. Mrs. Barnes committed suicide near Neversink, Sullivan county. (Bloomville (Del. Co.) Mirror).

1485. Cowan and Shelly, of Danville and Stanford, Lincoln co., Ky., dueled a few days since. Shelly died.

1486. John Smith died on Sunday last, at the Rondout Hotel. He was apparently over 70. (Rondout Examiner).

1487. The wife and 3 children of a Fourth Ward Policeman named Colgan died in a fire this morning at 102 Cherry st. Margaret Logan also died. (NY Evening Post, Saturday).

1488. A son of Philip Ogsbury, of Guilderland, died of hydrophobia, on Saturday.

May 22, 1852
1489. David Kennison died on the 24th of Feb., in Chigaco, aged 116 years, 3 months and 7 days. He was in the Boston tea party.

1490. A son of Mr. William Spendley, of
Binghampton, about 13, living with his uncle,
Richard Spendley, at Smithboro, was killed on
Tuesday last.

1491. The Providence Journal announces the death
of William Wilkinson, in his 92nd year, the oldest
living graduate of Brown University. He was
engaged in Sullivan's expedition during the
revolutionary war.

1492. The venerable lady of the Hon. John Quincy
Adams, died at Washington on Saturday last, over
77.

1493. On Friday the 7th, two children of David
Hoke, of Berwick township, Adams county, Pa., were
burnt to death.

1494. A few days since, Joseph Johnson, aged 93, a
revolutionary soldier, died at Pleasant Mills. He
entered the service in 1776, when only 16.

1495. The family Blye, consisting of 10 persons,
living one mile below Patriot, Ind., were poisoned
to death. (Cincinnati Courier).

1496. On Friday morning the steamer Troy was run
into while passing Blue Point, near Poughkeepsie.
Thomas Foot, colored, was drowned off the
steamer.

1497. William T. Pullen died on the 19th inst., at
Providence.

1498. On Saturday last, William Gilrowe drowned at
Rondout, aged 26 or 27.

1499. Daniel Kelly died near 50th street on
Saturday last. (NY Express).

                    May 29, 1852
1500. Drowned last Friday in Kingston, a 2 year
old daughter of George Brown. (Kingston
Journal).

1501. Joseph W. Gorgus, of Harrisburg, Pa., was
lately killed near Nashville, Tenn.

1502. A sail boat was capsized near New Bedford on
May 24th. The son of Jonathan Howland and the son
of Tileston Wood were drowned.

1503. The venerable George Howland died on Friday at his residence in New Bedford, aged about 70.

1504. Judge Anthony M. Van Bergen died on Sunday, in his 58th year. (Coxsackie Union).

1505. William Sawyer, Esq., of Charlestown, his 5 year old daughter and a man named Ames were killed by a train at West Cambridge. (Boston Post, 26th).

1506. Charles Thayer, a brakeman, was killed at Attica on Friday last, aged 20.

1507. A man named Basher, was killed while trying to cross the track near Salem, Washington co. (Troy Whig).

1508. The wife and child of Patrick Kiernan, of this village, were burned last Monday and died yesterday. (Coxsackie Union).

1509. The body of John Smith was picked up in the river opposite this place on Tuesday of this week. He was missing last fall.

1510. Joseph Blair, 26 or 28, a native of Montreal, Canada, where parents and 2 brothers survive, drowned between Ellenville and New York on the canal, on the 21st inst. (Journal).

1511. Wallace, son of Chauncey Goodrick, of this village, about 8, drowned on the 18th inst., in the pond on Hasbrouck avenue.

1512. The body of Robert Emerson, who was drowned in the Rondout stream, 2 miles above Napanoch some 2 months ago, was found on Sunday of last week. (Ellenville Journal).

1513. John Howard Payne, Esq., author of the popular song 'Home Sweet Home', has died. (Baltimore Patriot).

June 5, 1852

1514. We learn from the New York papers that one of the boilers of the Steamboat Eastern City, lying at the foot of Grand street, exploded on Saturday afternoon, killing Capt. Sterns, engineer Curtis, Charles Gorman, Francis Mayo and Charles Hall.

1515. Died on Saturday last, Matthew J. Myers, a prominent citizen of this village, in his 53rd year. (Poughkeepsie American).

1516. On Sunday morning last, a young man named Arthur W. Blanchard, 21, a baker in this village, was drowned at the mouth of the Creek, in the Hudson River. He was a native of Dorsetshire, England. (Catskill Democrat).

June 12, 1852
1517. Jun 7, in this village, Charles Hoytt, son of Dilazon and Jane M. Burhans, aged 2 years, 4 months and 14 days.

1518. May 29, Flatbush, Mary M., daughter of Stephen Weeks, in her 18th year.

1519. Jun 1, in this town, Francis Marion, son of Josiah and Anna Maria Smith, 3 years, 8 months and 12 days old.

1520. In Toronto, on Friday last, a woman named Donnely, while feeding her cow, was gored by the animal and almost instantly killed.

1521. Mr. Edward Stevenson, son of Rev. Evan Stevenson, of Georgetown, Ky., was lately killed in that place by Alexander Carrick, of Scott county.

1522. Franklin Pierce was born in NH in about 1805 to the late Benjamin Pierce who was a revolutionary officer and Governor of NH in 1827. Franklin was elected to Congress in 1833 and was Colonel of the New England Regiment in the Mexican War. He is married with 3 children.

1523. On Monday of last week, a little boy named James Norton was accidently drowned. (Poughkeepsie Telegraph).

1524. On Friday last, Mrs. Elizabeth Richardson, residing 9 miles back of Covington, was killed by a snake. (Louisville Journal).

1525. A Canada paper records the death of Mr. Chas. Boucher of Berthier, District of Montreal, aged 106. He was married three times and had 60 children.

June 19, 1852

1526. Daniel Webster was born at Salisbury, NH, Jan 18, 1782, and is in his 71st year.

1527. Gen. Winifeld Scott was born near Petersburg, Virginia, June 13, 1786, and is now 66.

1528. Royal Beach, a Vermonter, hung humself last week.

1529. A duel was fought on the 2d inst., at Fort Mello, Florida, between Col. Grouard and Major Jones, of Hopkins, who was killed. Bowie knives were used.

1530. Tuesday afternoon, John Roach, a laborer employed in the Sugar House, in Vandam st., was prostrated from the heat. He died in the Hospital.

1531. The whaleship Lawrence, of Poughkeepsie, was lost on a reef off the coast of Japan on 28 May 1846. Two of the 3 life boats were never heard from, the 3d reached the Island of Japan where they were confined for 13 months. Williams, of the crew, was murdered. (NY Express).

June 26, 1852

1532. Mr. Bond, of Vermont, had his funeral sermon prepared and read to him before he died.

1533. Frederick Shilling, who was committed a few days ago by Mayor Fleming, of Alleghany, Pa., died in the county jail on Saturday last.

1534. Mr. Enos Humphrey, who was a dyer in a wool factory near Staunton, V., fell into a vat and was scalded to death.

1535. Two boys of Thomas Finney, of Halifax Township, Pa., were killed by lightning last week.

1536. A young man named Alfred Beard met with a horrid death at East Rush, Monroe co., on Wednesday, leaving a wife and 2 children.

1537. The wife and boy, aged 12, of Mr. Arthur Mc Narny were drowned at Rhinebeck on Tuesday.

1538. A boy named George Fisher, whose parents reside near Port Jervis, was drowned in the canal near that place on the 6th inst.

1539. News has lately been received in New York of the death of David Graham, a distinguished lawyer of that city, in Italy.

1540. Died in this village on the 16th inst., John Armstrong, Counsellor at Law, aged 57, son of Gen. John Armstrong, born in the town of Red Hook. (Rhinebeck Mechanic).

1541. A letter from Sault Ste. Marie dated May 27th mentions the death of one Sarah nee Hynes, in her 28th year, a native of England, who was married to an Indian named Cadotte.

July 3, 1852

1542. Jun 16, Simpson's Tannery, Shandaken, Thos. Brady, about 30, leaving a wife and four children. (Ulster Republican).

1543. Schidel, who shot Waider, a deputy constable in St. Louis last October, has been sentenced to jail.

1544. Henry Clay, died on Tuesday last.

1545. On Saturday last, Samuel Best, a deckhand, fell off the R. L. Stevens, near Hastings, and drowned. Deceased was from Columbia county.

July 10, 1852

1546. Some of the negroes of Mr. James E. Houston, of Mc Intosh Co., Ga., have confessed that they murdered their master, who has been missing one week.

1547. Henry Clay was born on April 12, 1777 in Hanover county, Virginia.

1548. Adams and Belisle, convicted of murder in N. Orleans, were hanged on the 2d inst.

1549. Jul 5, New Orleans, the steamer St. James exploded. Killed were Judge Isaac Preston, of the Supreme Court, and Mr. Woolf, the Corporation Attorney, and others.

1550. Herman T. Livingston, formerly of Rondout, was drowned with 2 others on May 29th in Calif.

1551. The 5 year old son of Wm. Adams, of Glasco, drowned on the 6th inst.

July 17, 1852
1552. Jun 8, San Francisco, Hiram Yates, 22, formerly of this village.

1553. On Wednesday of last week, Samuel Jones, a farmer of Arkwright, was killed at the house of Mrs. Morey, southeast of Dunkirk.

1554. John Abby, Jr., of Colchester, Delaware Co., is missing. The Sullivan County Whig of the 6th says his body was found in Basket Pond, Callicoon.

1555. Matthias Rote, about 45, of the town of Livingston, cut his throat on Jun 30th and died on the 3rd inst. (Hudson Republican).

1556. Jeremiah Clearwater is indicted for the murder of his brother Andrew.

July 31, 1852
1557. Wm. Gallagher and Anthony Mc Call of Moyamensing, wagered over liquor consumption. Gallagher has since died.

The Steamer Henry Clay caught fire on the 28th, two and a half miles below Yonkers during a race: A list of the bodies recovered and recognized follows: <#'s 1558-1587>

1558. Mathew Cransell, 3d, 12 month old son of Mathew Cransell, Jr., of Albany.

1559. Christopher Benjamin Hill, 13, colored of Wooster st., NY.

1560. Mrs. A. Fennel, wife of Owen Fennel, of Wilmington, NC, found at Fort Lee.

1561. R. A. Sands, infant son of Isaac Sands, of 85 Stanton st.

1562. George F. Whitlock, house agent, of 96 Allen st., NY, and wife.

Deaths in the Henry Clay disaster:

1563. Miss Adeline M. Holmes, 96 Allen st., NY

1564. Miss Elizabeth M. Hillman, of Troy, 86

1565. Mrs. Harriet E. Colby, wife of Stoddard B.
Colby of Montpelier, Vt., aged 31.

1566. Mrs. Emily Bartlett, wife of Prof. Bartlett
of the Collegiate Institute, Poughkeepsie.

1567. Mrs. Maria Bailey, wife of Prof. Bailey of
West Point, and her daughter Maria, 16 years old.

1568. Mary Thompson, 10 and Eugene Thompson, 6
weeks, children of John S. Thompson, District
Attorney of Lancaster Co., Pa.

1569. John Hosier of 214 Wooster st., NY, about
18.

1570. Elizabeth Pearsall of East Brooklyn, LI,
aged 15.

1571. Wm. M. Ray, his wife Abby Ann Ray, and
Caroline Ray, of Cincinnati.

1572. Julia Hoy of Newburgh, aged 18.

1573. Mrs. M. Wadsworth, aged 26, of Fishkill.

1574. Mrs. S. Dennison of West Farms, aged 60.

1575. Miss M. Cooper of West Farms, about 35.

1576. Geo. K. Marcher of 18 Eleventh st., aged
38.

1577. Johanna Byard Marsden Handforth, aged 17
months.

1578. Mary A. Robinson, wife of A. Robinson of 69
Perry st., and Isabella, their daughter, aged 1.

1579. Charlotte Johnson, colored, of
Poughkeepsie.

1580. Mrs. J. Murray, wife of Adam Murray of
Chicago, Ill., aged 30 and a child aged 1.

Deaths in the Henry Clay disaster:

1581. Margaret Chatillon, wife of G. Chatillon, C. Chatillon, aged 3 and H. Chatillon, 14 months.

1582. Geo. Thielman, 31, of Poughkeepsie.

1583. Mrs. A. C. Barcroft, wife of S. C. Barcroft of Philadelphia, aged 58.

1584. Stephen Allen, lawyer, of New York.

1585. Mr. Downing of Newburgh, accomplished horticulturist and author.

1586. Ten bodies are unidentified. One has a handkerchief with the name J. J. Speed of Baltimore.

1587. Missing, in the Henry Clay disaster include, Miss Catharine Dewint, of Fishkill; Mrs. Hannah B. Marcher of 18 Eleventh St.; Mrs. Marsden Handforth of NY city; the child and nurse of Elmore Thompson of 180 Henry st., NY; Mrs. Simmons, wife of J. W. Simmons of 67 Eldridge st., one child and a servant; Isaac D. Sands of 86 Stanton st., NY and Mrs. B. Williams, of Poughkeepsie.

1588. Judge Sanford died at Toledo on the 28th inst.

August 7, 1852
1589. Ann Hoag and Jonas Williams were hung in Poughkeepsie on Friday last.

1590. Additional deaths from the Henry Clay, Mr. J. S. Schoonmaker, merchant, of Jordanville, his wife and niece Miss Jordan, eldest daughter of Selah T. Jordan, Esq., of the same place. Also Matilda Wadsworth. (Dem.).

1591. Capt. E. Williams expired after being bitten six weeks ago by a rabid dog, at Wilmington, Del.

1592. Among the deaths in Rochester by the prevailing epidemic is that of Moses H. Seward.

1593. Capt. Marcy and his command of 80 men have been massacred by Indians. (Fort Smith Herald, Jul 17th).

1594. Aug 9, Boscobel, Westchester County, Julia M., wife of Henry B. Livingston, in her 25th year.

1595. Aug 6, New York, of typhoid fever, Doct. L. R. Brodhead, aged 38, burial in Rhinebeck.

1596. Henry Van Dyck, of Coxsackie, about 21, hung himself on the 1st inst.

1597. Mr. Daniel Haight, of Fishkill, was recently choked to death, while at dinner, by a piece of meat.

1598. Mr. Peter Adriance, of East Fishkill, died on Wednesday of wounds inflicted by a mowing machine.

1599. Hon. Jabez P. Thompson, coalition Senator from Plymouth, Mass., hung himself in a barn at his residence in Halifax on the 10th inst.

1600. Mr. Basil Mc Knew, chief engineer of the Chemical Works, located on the city docks, fell into the machinery and was killed.

1601. At Truxton, in Courtland county, on the 3d instant, a man named O'Donoghue, 55, killed Mrs. Daniel Kinny.

1602. At Darien, Georgia, in the latter part of July, James Houston, unmarried, was murdered by many workmen on his plantation.

1603. A story about the afflicted family of Prof. Kingsley, without other names, is printed.

1604. Two more identified dead from the Henry Clay disaster on the 28th ultimo, William Mc Clusky, and a Miss Smith, sister of Hill, of Philadelphia.

1605. Robert Rantoul, Jr., a Member of the House of Representatives from Mass., died in Washington city last Sunday morning of acute erysipelas.

1606. Captain Marcy may have been massacred with his command, by Indians, last week.

1607. The Ellenville Journal says that Thomas Edwards and his wife, of that place, were on the

ill-fated Henry Clay at the time of her loss and
are presumed drowned.

August 21, 1852

1608. Miss Skinner was drowned, says the Niagara
correspondent of the Springfield Republican.

1609. Mr. Amos E. Frey of Missouri was recently
killed by Indians. (Calif. news).

1610. A man by the name of Shannon was hung by the
people of Shasta, for the murder of a man named
Taucalin. (Calif. news).

1611. Joseph Hartman, who keeps a grocery on East
Genessee st., Buffalo, was murdered by robbers on
Monday morning.

1612. A man named Darrow murdered his wife, who
died on Monday at Buffalo.

1613. The Boston Transcript says that the three
daughters of Rev. Joseph Marsh were terribly
burned by the explosion of a can of 'burning
fluid'.

1614. Mrs. General Taylor, relict of the late
President, died at East Pascagoula on Saturday.

1615. The NY Day Book of Thursday says that Mr.
Harper, of Augusta, Ga., was found dead in his bed
yesterday morning at the Astor House.

1616. The massacre of Capt. Marcy is confirmed.

August 28, 1852

1617. Aug 18, town of Rock, Wisconsin, Peter
Weidman, formerly of this place, in his 62nd
year.

1618. President Louis attended Count D'Orsay's
funeral. (European news).

1619. Gen. Scott received a telegraphic dispatch
from Capt. Marcy, on the 24th inst., announcing
his safe arrival at Red River.

1620. James Maher, Irishman, died at Albany on the
23d inst., aged 74. He organized and commanded
the 'Irish Greens' in the war of 1812.

130

1621. We learn from the Poughkeepsie American that Andrew Mc Lean, of that place, committed suicide, leaving a wife and child.

1622. A report is now current that Capt. Stevenson, with officers and 56 men, have been killed by Camanches about 40 miles from Fort Belknap.

September 4, 1852
1623. Aug 30, in this village, Menett, daughter of Horace and Mary Eliza Miner, 1 year, 7 months and 2 days old.

1624. The Duke of Hamilton, the Senior Peer of Scotland, is dead. (European news).

1625. At Contra Casta, Mr. Johnson, the Sheriff, was killed in an Indian uprising. (Calif. news).

1626. A man named Welter, of Port Jervis, was killed near Turner's Station, on the Erie Railroad, on Thursday last.

1627. Edward Hunt, 8, son of Mr. John Hunt, of Williamsburgh, was run over by a train of cars at Forrestville, Conn. on Monday last.

1628. Enos Hays was found dead in a bed at the tavern of John O. Cole, in the village of Peekskill, on Thursday last.

1629. The 18 year old son of Mr. John Southard, of Ghent, was killed on Thursday last at the Ghent Station.

1630. A child of Mrs. S. Wyman Stoddard died at Farmingham, Me., last week.

1631. Matthew Raynor, who resides near Raleigh, died at the residence of Mr. Beard in Tipton County. Buried at his residence on Sunday. (Memphis (Tenn.) Enquirer).

1632. James Wool, another of the heros of the Revolution, died on Wednesday near Troy, on the farm where his father lived and died.

1633. Prof. Kingsley, a member of the Faculty of Yale College, died on the 31st ult., in New Haven. Born in Windham, Conn.

September 11, 1852

1634. Sep 6, Kiskatom, Nelly, relict of the late
Anthony Abeele, about 62.

1635. Aug 29, Glasco, Harman Whitaker, in his 50th
year.

Sep 7, The Steamship 'Reindeer'. The Reindeer
left NY at 7 o'clock this morning and arrived in
Malden at 1:15. She had just landed when the pipe
exploded. There were 179 passengers aboard when
the boat docked, 10 got off before the accident.
33 hands. The following people were killed through
6 o'clock Friday afternoon, Sep 10th.

1636. Frederick Monell, Barkeeper, remains taken
to Poughkeepsie (his place of residence) Saturday
night by HRRR.

1637. Francis or Fred Dunn, fireman, buried at
Malden.

1638. Peter Fouche, waiter, buried at Malden.

1639. John Bowers, waiter, buried at Malden.

1640. Robert Farrell, waiter, buried at Malden.

1641. Jacob Koche, waiter, buried at Malden.

1642. German waiter, name unknown, buried at
Malden.

1643. Solomon Savoy, colored, taken to Rhinebeck
(his place of residence) Saturday night by HRRR.

1644. John Savoy, do do do.

1645. Dennis Savoy, do do do.

1646. James Brown, said to be a Cashier in a Bank
in Wall st., NY. His remains are in charge of
Captain Farnham.

1647. Mrs. Mary Ann Bowers, wife of Daniel N.
Bowers, 916 Broadway, Albany. Remains taken to
Albany Sunday morning by steamer Chelsea. Her
husband, who is badly scalded, accompanied her.

1648. Norman P. Williamson, son of Rev. George R.
Williamson, of Amity, Saratoga County. His
remains are in a private vault, at Malden.

Deaths in the Reindeer disaster:

1649. John G. Rumfeldt, employee of the Danish Consul, private vault.

1650. D. F. Holdrige, 79 Eagle st., Albany, where his remains were taken on board the Chelsea.

1651. Thomas J. Barnes, Richmond, Va.

1652. Hugh Rileigh of Richmond, Va., and his step-daughters, Margaretta and Samuella Andrews. Their remains were deposited in a private vault in Malden. Mr. Rileigh made his will before he died.

1653. H. Beach Cox, 2nd Engineer. Remains sent to New York on Sunday, by steamer South American.

1654. James Brown, deck hand.

1655. Estelle Loop, daughter of John Loop, of the firm of Warren, Loop and Bliss, New York city. She was about 12 years old. Her remains were taken to Hudson.

1656. Garwood Benway, stewart, Pine Plains. His remains are in charge of the Captain of the boat.

1657. Mrs. Sarah N. Lockwood, of Albany.

1658. Augustus W. Whipple, of Cambridge, Mass.

1659. Rev. George R. Williamson, of Amity, Saratoga Co. His remains were taken to New York this morning by HRRR in charge of his father and father-in-law.

1660. David N. Bower died on the steamer Chelsea, yesterday, on his way to Albany.

1661. Edward Ziller, a German, died at the Malden House at 5 1/4 o'clock this morning.

1662. Wm. H. Snell, Richmond, Va., remains removed by his friends.

1663. Wood Baker, of Princeton, NJ. His friends are at Malden, and will probably remove his remains.

1664. Joseph Ebinger, a waiter on board the boat, died at the Malden House on Tuesday.

1665. Those still alive: Hugh Lowrey of Newburgh, bad; Miss Lockwood, of Albany, daughter of Mrs. SNL, badly scalded, but may recover. John Howlett, 1st engineer, doing well. Mr. & Mrs. Quigley, latter very badly scalded. J. E. Lockwood, son of Mrs. SNL of Albany, may recover. Charles Mc Gregor and Henry C. Flick who will recover. Mrs. Geo. W. Williamson, badly scalded, cannot recover.

September 18, 1852
1666. Sep 11, Malden, Caroline E., wife of Edward Bigelow, Esq., and daughter of David Boies, Esq., of Blandford, Mass., 38 years old.

1667. Sep 12, Hunter's Island, Westchester County, Hon. John Hunter, in his 73rd year.

Update on the Reindeer accident:

1668. Miss Lockwood, of Albany died Tuesday. Her remains were taken home by her friends, Wednesday.

1669. Mrs. Amy Williamson, wife of Rev. Geo. R. Williamson, of Amity, died Wednesday morning. Her remains were taken to New York the same day.

1670. Hugh Lowrie, of Newburgh, died Wednesday morning.

1671. Mr. Quigley died yesterday (Friday) morning at 5 o'clock.

Nearly recovered in the Reindeer disaster:

1672. L. E. Lockwood, of Albany, who was considerably scalded, accompanied his sister's remains home yesterday. He will probably recover.

1673. Captain Hoyt and wife are said to be suffering from the effects of their injuries, at their residence in Hudson, but no danger of death is apprehended.

1674. John Howlett, first Engineer of the boat is doing well.

1675. Charles Mc Gregor, of Brooklyn, has gone home and is rapidly recovering.

1676. Henry C. Flick has also left Malden, convalescing.

1677. Additional deaths from the Henry Clay disaster include Abraham Crist and A. J. Downing.

1678. Joel Woodbeck, a resident of Nassau, was killed at Berlin on Saturday evening. (Troy Times, 6th). <The Telegraph of the 25th says his name was Whitbeck>

1679. Samuel Ward, colored, was executed at Newcastle, Del., on the 8th inst., for the murder of George A. Davidson, in May last.

1680. A man named Redding killed Christiana Kramer in Cincinnati on the 4th inst., then cut his own throat.

1681. Andrew Norris, a soldier of the Revolution, who was with Washington at the time of the execution of Major Andre, is still living in Cincinnati, aged 90 years and 5 months.

1682. Mr. Calvin Couch, of Montgomery, was burned and died when a camphene lamp exploded.

1683. Mr. Flynn, of Lockport, died when his wagon overturned on Monday night. Wife and children survived the upset.

1684. At Nunda village, Dr. Warner and his father-in-law died on the 4th and 5th inst., of a disease called cholera by attending physicians.

1685. David C. Brush, Editor of the Suffolk Democrat, published at Huntington, died on the 6th inst., in his 44th year.

1686. Hon. Mark H. Sibley died at Canandaigua on the 8th inst.

September 25, 1852
1687. Sep 20, in this town, John Gillespy, aged 7 years, 7 months and 2 days.

1688. Woods Baker died in the Reindeer explosion on the 7th inst., in his 29th year, son of Elias and Hetty W. Baker. (Democratic (Pa.) Standard).

1689. Mr. Taylor, a shoe maker, of Natick, Mass., was murdered in his own house on the 17th inst.

1690. David Gorman killed his wife near Cincinnati last week.

1691. A son of Mr. Robert Pye, of Cincinnati, died of lockjaw a few days ago.

1692. Miss Phoebe Ann Quigley, 30, one of the Reindeer passengers, died at Malden on Sunday last. Mr. Thomas Quigley, who died last week, was about 60 and owned a plantation at St. John's in Puerto Rico.

October 2, 1852
1693. Sep 28, Kingston, Miss Amelia Vredenburgh, 22 years old.

1694. Sep 29, in this village, Paul Snyder, aged 75.

1695. Last Friday, Kingston, Mr. John Vanderlyn, painter. A native of Kingston, interred at Wiltwyck Cemetery.

1696. Died, in this city, on the 19th inst., James Copland Mason, 30, who married Miss Margaret Atkinson about a year since with Jenny Lind as a bridesmaid and Otto Goldschmidt as groomsman. (Buffalo Cour.).

1697. Brevet Major Roland, aged 35, Captain of the Second Regiment of Artillery, died of yellow fever on Tuesday at Castle Pinckney, Charleston Harbor.

1698. Ex-Governor Badger, of NH, died at Gilmantown on Wednesday, of disease of the brain, aged 73 years, 8 months.

1699. The Duke of Wellington, conqueror of Napoleon, expired at Walmer Castle, on Tuesday the 14th inst.

October 9, 1852
1700. James Whitcomb, United States Senator of Indiana, died in New York on the 5th inst.

October 16, 1852
1701. Oct 4, John W. Kiersted, infant son of Maria A. and John Kiersted, Jr., 11 months.

1702. Oct 11, in this village, Mrs. Maria, wife of E. J. Mc Carthy, Esq., in her 38th year.

1703. Two brothers named Davis were killed in a gambling fight at Norfolk in 1806.

1704. In Havana, two angels, the beautiful children of Idelfonso and Francisco Valdes have fled to the bosom of the Eternal. Glory to them.

October 23, 1852
1705. Oct 20, Blue Point, on the Hudson, Robert Kerr, about 19, of Glasco, drowned. Parents survive in Glasco.

1706. John M. W. Lace, well known in this city, was shot to death by Ann Wheeler, an American, formerly of Cleveland. (Milwaukie Wis., 14th).

1707. Solomon Dunford drowned on the 26th, at West Cowes, Isle of Wight.

---, Cecily 742
   Diamond 1183 George
   1248 Henry 1131 Jack
   46 Napoleon 1699
   Reuben 1359 Seaman
   1419 Vincent 1219
ABBOT, Mrs 453
ABBY, John 1554
ABEELE, Anthony 1634
   Nelly 1634
ACKERLY, Henry 1120
ACKERMAN, John 238
ACKERT, Morgan 858
ADAMS, --- 1548 C 150
   Catherine L 827 Chalora
   J 1314 Charles Francis
   10 John 789 973 John Q
   789 1313 1492 Parmelia
   A 1312 Phebe Ann 1315
   Samuel 613 Wm 1551
ADDINGTON, Mr 231
ADLER, --- 1026
   Nathan 968
ADRIANCE, Peter 1598
AIKIN, Asenath 1126
   Charles 1126
   William H 1126
ALDHONSON, S 1227
ALLARD, Armenia 962
   Emeline 962 Thomas 962
ALLCORN, Joseph 171
ALLEMAN, John 505
ALLEN, Eliza 1229 J.
   Hart 706 John 110 1215
   Stephen 1584 Wm 628
ALLEY, Jacob 827
   Mehitable 827
   Washington 827
AMES, --- 1505
ANDERSON, Jeremiah 142
   Mr. 381 Wm H 931
ANDLEAS, Nicholas 998
ANDRE, Major 1681
ANDREWS, Margaretta 1652
   Samuella 1652
   Thomas 612
ANTONIA, Maurice 1467
ARBUCKLE, General 1430
ARMOR, --- 520
ARMSTRONG, John 1540
ARRIG, William 168

ARTMAN, John 817
ATKINSON, Margaret 1696
AUCHMOODY, Louis 104
AUDUBON, John James
   1027
AUSTIN, Charles 145
BACKUS, Mrs 818
BADGER, Governor 1698
BAHAN, Albert 968 1026
   John 1026
BAILEY, Maria 1567
   Prof 1567
BAIN, Mary 656
BAKER, Ambrose 1329
   Benjamin F 446 Elias
   1688 Hetty W 1688 Mrs
   455 R J R 1392 Woods
   1663 1688 Zenus W 455
BALDWIN, Dorcas 1416
   Goodrich 1416 James W
   1339 John H 1339
   Joseph Morris 1225
   Major 929 Margaret
   Lavinia 1416 Maria
   Woodward 211
   Rodney N 211
BALL, Elijah 107
BANCROFT, Mr 813
BANGE, Mary S 861
   Wm B 861
BARBER, Ezra 989 Orbin
   682 William 682
BARBOUR, Dr 319
BARCLAY, Catharine 1006
   Henry 987 1006 1012
   Thomas 1012
BARCROFT, A C 1583
   S C 1583
BARGIS, M E 317
BARKER, Cyrus 680
   P Byron 397
BARNARD, Sarah 1341
BARNES, Mrs 1484
   Thomas J 1651
BARNETT, George 774
BARNITZ, Charles A 614
BARNUM, --- 923
BARRE, David 478
BARRELL, Theodore 1330
BARRET, Jane 766
BARRY, Richard 1073

BARTLE, Catharine 1137
  Valentine 1137
BARTLETT, Emily 1566
  Prof 1566
BARTON, Able 609 James
  609 Minerva 609 Mr 609
  Plint 1088 Sally 609
BASCOMB, Bishop 860
BASHER, --- 1507
BASTIAN, George 351
BATES, George O 45
BAY, S. Mansfield 285
BEACH, Ebenezer 599
  Royal 1528
BEAN, Mr 1361
BEAR, Henry 646
BEARD, Alfred 1536
  Mr 1631
BEATTY, Eliza 1241
  William 1241
BEAVER, John 196
BECK, George W 958
BECKLEY, James 477
  Susanna 477
BEEBE, Nathan J 1244
BEECHER, Dr 1372
BEEKMAN, John 421
BEERS, Adeline 877
  Henry N 877
BELISLE, --- 1548
BELKNAP, Daniel 924
  Ebenezer 1464
  General 1430
BELL, Governor 991 Isaac
  515 John 510
BELZHOOVER, Melchoir 874
BEM, General 559
BENEDICT, James 1169
  Mary Amelia 1169
BENJAMEN, Joseph 655
BENNETT, Thomas 539
BENSON, E T 1231
BENTON, Albert S 312
BENWAY, Garwood 1656
BERNHOEFF, --- 1428
BESEMER, Casper 1207
  Jane 1208
BESSTON, Capt 497
BEST, Samuel 1545
BETTS, Isaac C 58 John 58
BEUZEVILLE, Geo 225
BEVANS, Henry 1248

BEVIER, Anna 730
  Wilhelmus 730
BEVINS, John J 232
BEZLY, Almira 1280
BICKFORD, William 1030
BIDDY, Jonathan 486
BIGELOW, Asa 550 877
  Caroline E 1666
  Edward 1666
BIRCH, W S 916
BIRD, Mrs 754
BISHOP, John 1446
BISPHAM, John E 92
BLACK, Edward J 387
  James A 6 John 486
  Peter 486
BLACKNEY, Francis 622
BLAIR, Joseph 1510
BLAKE, Dr 834
  Jerry 1246
BLANCHARD, Arthur 1516
BLAND, Hiram 940
BLANEY, Nathaniel B 132
BLEEKER, Harmanus 276
BLESS, Michael 463
BLESSENE, Michael 463
BLISS, George 1131
BLUM, Robert 1327
BLYE, --- 1495
BOCARME, Count 1184
BOGARDUS, Elizabeth
  Arnold 1365 J K 1365
  Maria D W 196
  Solomon 196
BOIES, David 1666
BOLT, John 1009
BOND, A 711 Mr 1532
BONDALL, Mr 800
BONEL, James 869
BONNER, George 120
BONNET, Thomas 1035
BOOKOUT, Mr 1451
BOOKSTAVER, John L 89
BOOTH, John 1128 Mary A
  400 Mary Elizabeth
  400 Thomas 400
BORDENHAVE, --- 1382
BOSTON, David 740
BOSTWICK, George 32
  Mr 1397
BOUCHER, Chas 1525
BOWEN, Ephraim 185

CAMPBELL, Alex 880
Donald 919 Emma 352
George 143 John 1131
Lucy Ann 353 Mr 582
Wm M 501
CANEDO, Juan de Dios 658
CARAY, Patrick 575
CAREY, Stephen C 1173
CARLOCK, Officer 1389
CARMAN, Wm C 930
CARPENTER, Jacob 1040
Thomas 920 1459
CARR, Esek 569 750 Mr
607 Mrs 1254
CARRAGAN, Matthew 1143
CARRICK, Alexander 1521
CARRIGAN, --- 1324
Matthew 1230
CARROLL, --- 605 1440
CARSON, Catharine 1060
1111 William James 551
CASE, Mrs 679 Wm W 999
CASS, Hiram 524
CASSEL, James 634
CATALINI, Madam 235
CATT, Michael 1480
CAVERY, Luke 1340
CAVONY, Mary 1340
CHAMBERLAIN, John D 120
CHAMBERS, Samuel 1212
CHAMPLIN, William 745
CHANDLER, --- 606
John 619
CHAPIN, Gad N 642
CHAPMAN, George A 1092
J 743
CHARBONNEAU, John 975
Louis 975
CHASE, Mr 810 Thomas 318
CHATILLON, C 1581 G 1581
H 1581 Margaret 1581
CHEEVER, Marie 827
CHIN-CHI-KE, --- 1386
CHITTENDON, Nathaniel
1007
CHONTEAU, Pierre 282
CHUCK-A-PE, --- 866
CHURCHHOUSE, John 1033
CHURCHILL, Mr 1382
CLAPP, Henry C 800
CLAPPER, Jacob 52
Zachariah 52

CLAPPERTON, James 59
CLARK, --- 395 1110
Edmund 112 Ira 882
Jno 897 Joseph 937
Samuel 1272
CLARKE, Albert H 928
CLAUSEN, E 1246
CLAY, Cassius M 202
H 603 Henry 644 1461
1544 1547 James 757
Porter 603 Rodney
Baldwin 1242
CLAYPOLE, David C 79
CLAYTON, Charles M 30
J M 1064 John Fisher
1064 John M 30
CLEARWATER, Abraham
1085 Andrew 1556
Jeremiah 1085 1556
John 1085 Kitty 1085
CLEMENT, Moses 712
CLEMENTS, --- 1005
James 1231 1262
CLEVELAND, --- 1194
CLINTON, De Witt 924
CLORE, Edmund 920
CLOUGH, Henry Franklin
704 Isaac S 704
COATES, Jonathan 753
COBB, George 1226
Warren 1449
COCKEY, M G 466
COE, Charles 553
George 553 L 1403
Thomas D 553
COFFIN, J B 189
COIR, William 627
COLBY, Harriet E 1565
Stoddard B 1565
COLE, --- 1263 Jesse
395 John O 1628
P Elmendorf 1373
William H 831
COLEMAN, Frank 555
Hannah 555 John 820
Obed M 350
COLGAN, --- 1487
COLLINS, Ellen 705
COLMAN, Samuel 856
COLTON, Walter 1022
COLVOY, James 105
Margaret 105

COMSTOCK, Deacon 912
CONKLIN, Mr 380
CONN, Thomas 162
CONNOR, Captain 518
    James 109 1450
    Peter 109
CONOLY, Catharine 1340
CONQUEST, Wm 1304
CONVEY, Bridget 1053
COOK, --- 287 George W
    484 Louis P 81
COOLEY, Charles 426
    Daniel M 362 John 426
COOLIDGE, V P 173
COON, Abraham 354
    Elizabeth 36 Jemima
    1125 1156 John H 36
    Robert 1125 1156
    William H 837
COOPER, --- 702
    Commodore 721 Emily
    405 James Fennimore
    1299 1354 M 1575
    Susan Augusta 1299
    Thomas A 126
COPLEY, George W 1346
CORBEN, Charles 83
CORBITT, James 460
CORNELIUS, Philip 1000
CORNELL, Thomas W 1278
CORNISH, Captain 46
COSDEN, Mrs 1069
COUCH, Calvin 1682
COULIN, Terace 526
COULT, W 966
COWAN, --- 1485
COX, --- 454 Charles
    1219 H Beach 1653
    William H 1174
CRAFT, A 1393 Edith 1393
CRAGIN, Mary E 1229
CRANDALL, Horace 389
CRANE, Benjamin 39 John
    H 1482 S B 1482
CRANSE, George 1238
CRANSELL, Mathew 1558
CRAWFORD, Catherine 770
    Elijah 371
    John 770 1061 1070
CRAWLEY, Lieut 847
CREHORE, Sarah 24
CRISMAN, William 1435

CRIST, Abraham 1677
CRITTENDEN, Mrs 1264
CROCKER, James 34
CROCKETT, David 1423
    Thos J 1423
CROGHAN, Col 18 General
    1430 Wm 894
CROMWELL, Oliver 79
CROSBY, Mary 981
CROW, Charles 237
CROZIER, Mrs 695
CULLEN, Josephine 1475
CULLEY, John 529
    William 529
CUMMERFORD, Henry 486
CURE, W 808
CURRAN, Harriet Emeline
    311 William 311
CURTIS, --- 1514
    Samuel A 937
CUSHEN, Charles 16
CUSHING, Mary 1414
CUTHBERT, E 926
CUTTER, B G 280
D'ORSAY, Count 1618
DAKIN, Hiram 1149
DALEY, Michael 556
DANA, Andrew 1201
DANIELS, Capt 1441
DANOON, Alexander 764
DARROW, --- 1612
DAVIDSON, George A 1679
DAVIS, --- 1703
    Christopher 20 Edward
    H 21 Ida Frances 253
    James 228 John 568
    John P 293 Joseph F
    253 Maria 293 1166
    Mary E 253 Mathew L
    748 Mr 659 1215 Thos
    F 1166 Wm H 875
DAWES, Jas 1178
DAWSON, Senator 629
DAY, Aaron 488
    Alonzo 441
DE BLOIS, Francis E 826
DE BOCARME, Hippolyte
    Visart 1236
DE GROFF, --- 864
DE LA TOUR, M Antoine
    Galland 1333

142

DE LIESSELINE, Francis
  Gottier 129
DE NOYELLES, Louis 1445
DEACON, John 1196
DEAN, James 33
DEARY, --- 945
DEAS, Edward 190 F A 303
DECKER, Cornelia Ann 731
  John 731 P M G 64
  Peter 64 Peter M 239
DEDERICK, Herman 1155
DEFOREST, Adelaide F 573
  Miss 231 William H 573
DEGROFF, Bernard V K
  1296 1297 Henry F 1296
  Margaret 1296 1297
  Sarah M 1297
DEITZ, Joseph P 887
DEMARET, Mr 1213
DEMEYER, John 1114
DEMYER, Dewitt C 1323
  John 1323
DENGLER, Daniel 816
DENISON, Elisha 436
DENMAN, Stephen 720
DENNISON, S 1574
DENNY, M P 204
DENTON, Christopher 1134
DEVAZAC, Major 1051
DEWEY, Thomas 124
DEWINT, Catharine 1587
DEWITT, --- 1289
  Elizabeth 427 James
  479 William C 427
DEXTER, Charles H 1441
DEYO, Daniel 257
DIAMOND, --- 1183
  James 1123
DICKENSON, Judge 1068
DICKERMAN, A 687
DICKESON, Emma 1294
DICKINSON, Col 459 Manco
  C 921 Senator 921
DILLARD, Thomas 807
DILLAWAY, Francis 802
DILLON, Mrs 210
DIMOND, Isaac 344
DINGLE, Samuel K 883
DIX, Col 19 John A 300
DIXON, Hugh 983 James 51
DOANE, A Sidney 1368
DOLAN, Jas 192

DOLE, Nelson 315
DOLTON, George 755
DONAVAN, James 844
DONNELY, --- 1520
DONOHUE, James 1249
DONOVAN, John 1468
  Timothy 1110
DOOLEY, John 575
DORLAN, Robert 697
  William 697
DORSEY, Thomas B 73
DOUGHERTY, John 213
  Leeds 101
DOUGLAS, Henry 1231
DOUGLASS, Mrs 1159
DOWNES, Patrick 690
DOWNING, A J 1677
  Mr 1585
DOWNS, Abel 1367
  George P 1257
DOYLE, James 307 Mr 247
DRAKE, Dr 319
DRISCOLL, Cornelius 588
DRUM, Edward 1277
DRYSDALE, George 570
DUBOIS, Caroline Louisa
  1043 Elanor 1405 Elena
  1043 Elijah 1043
  James 177
DUDLEY, Enos G 141
DUFF, James 1300
DUGGAN, Patrick 1240
DUMONT, Captain 805
DUNBAR, --- 907
  Reuben 977 1037
DUNCAN, Col 243
  General 1430
DUNFORD, Solomon 1707
DUNN, Francis 1637 Fred
  1637 Jeremiah 1021
  John 727 855
  Michael 727
DUNNE, John 266 Mrs 266
DUNNIVAN, Patrick 1151
DURHAM, George A 108
  Jonathan 108
DUTY, John 757
DYER, Thomas 367
EAST, Richard 746
EATON, Samuel 631
EBINGER, Joseph 1664
ECKERT, John L 890

ECKFELDT, Adam 1385
EDELIN, Walter 1090
EDGEWORTH, Maria 198
    Richard Lowell 198
EDMONSON, Reuben 1438
EDWARDS, Charles 632
    John 309
    Thomas 309 1607
EGBERT, Andrew 1146
EGLESTON, John Martin
    1463 Major 1463
    Matilda 1463
ELDER, Robert 1049
ELDERKIN, Noble S 649
ELLARSON, George 1464
ELLIOTT, Schuyler 905
ELLORE, J 671
ELMENDORF, Dumond 86
    Egbert 636 666 Eliza
    1157 Geo 1087 Helen
    666 John P 1157 Luther
    H 86 Mary Ann 1087
ELMORE, Senator 722
ELTING, Elizabeth 494
EMERSON, Robert 1512
EMIGH, George W 251
    Mary Adelia 251
EMOTT, James 630
ENDLE, Lewis 268
ENGLE, Samuel 1288
ENNIS, Elizabeth 700
    Joseph 700
ERNST, Dr 376
ERPENSTEIN, John 1380
ESTES, Abner 1048
    B 1048
EVANGELISTA, Signor 1197
EVANS, Robert 432
EVARTS, Calvin 983
EVERETT, Edward 10
FAGAN, --- 896
FAIRBANKS, Mr 1281
FALCHENMAKER, William 247
FARGO, F A 392
FARMER, Henry 270
FARRAR, Timothy 63
FARRELL, John 1340
    Robert 1640
FARRER, Dr 319
FAULK, James G 503
FAUSS, Agatha 904
FEATHERLY, Rufus 1133

FEATHERSON, James 193
FELTER, Alonzo D 572
FENNEL, A 1560 Owen 1560
FENWICK, Elizabeth T
    1106 John 1106
FERGUSON, Grant J 1055
    Hannah A 244
FETTER, Hiram 755
FIELD, Capt 1452
    Francis Edward 1071
    John 1071 Sarah M
    1071 William 885
FIERO, Christopher 1363
    Mary 1340 Peter P 1363
FIFE, J 90
FIGG, --- 835 John 838
FILLMORE, Pres 1262
FINCH, --- 1357
FINNEY, Thomas 1535
FINNY, Tom 865
FISH, Gov 272
FISHER, George 1538
FITCH, Andrew 45
FITZGIBBON, James 478
FITZPATRICK, John 1388
FLAHERTY, --- 1203
FLANDERS, Dr 952
FLEMING, Mayor 1533
FLICK, Henry C 1665
    1676
FLINT, William 170
FLOUGHEY, John 1291
FLOURNOY, Thomas 757
FLOUTON, Joseph 451
FLOYD, R H 409
FLYNN, James 47 Mr 1683
    Tom 214
FOLAND, J 70
FOOT, Thomas 1496
FOOTE, --- 898 Dr 297 H
    Leander 405 Olive 405
FORSAITH, W W 1015
FOSTER, Jonathan C 964
FOUCHE, Peter 1638
FOUGNIES, Gustave 1184
FOWLER, James 884
FRANCE, Abram 1351 H W
    623 1185 Hannah 438 Mr
    685 Philip 438 S P 623
FRANKLIN, John 1352
FREDERICK, Jerusha 1013
    John 1108

144

FREEMAN, A M 1182 Geo R
    752 John 757
FRELIGH, Lavina Eliza
    1018 Maria 1018
    Samuel P 1018
FRENCH, Capt 839 1003
    Parker 1102
FREY, Amos E 1609
FRITZ, Frederick 678
FROST, --- 396 J W 1202
    Samuel 40
FROTHINGHAM, Mr 10
FULLER, Margaret 790
    Samuel 826
    William 1240
FULLERTON, Halloway 465
    Judge 465 Wm 465
FULLMER, Charles L 1307
    Elizabeth 1307
    Jacob F 1307
FURNESS, Edmund 1457
GABTER, Angelrodt 119
GALE, M 616
GALLAGHER, James 981
    John 200 Wm 1557
GALLITIN, Albert 339
GARDINER, Wm K 663
GARDNER, William 749
GARL, James 512
GARLAND, Joshua 827
GARRITY, Margaret 1277
GAY, --- 741 Barnet 49
    Joseph G 49
GAYLARD, --- 419
GEIGER, Francis 7
GENTRY, Eli 609 Jane 609
GEORGE, Elizabeth 609
    Hannah 609 Mrs 1124
GERARD, Marshal 1479
GERMAN, John 1239
GEROW, Mary Ann 1233
GHERKIN, C H 1247
GIBBONS, Anna 349
    Elizabeth 349 Mary R
    349 W P 349
GIBBS, Ezra 946
GIBSON, Mr 1397
    Nicholas 1001
GIDNEY, Charles 462
    Chauncey B 462
GILBERT, Levi 965
GILLESPIE, William 739

GILLESPY, John 1371 1687
    Sarah S 1371
GILLET, James 117
GILLETT, Gilbert M 1366
    Sarah 1366
GILMORE, Addison 1008
GILROWE, William 1498
GLORE, Edmund 1459
GOBLE, --- 1355
GOLDSCHMIDT, Otto 1696
GOLDSTIEN, Moses 757
GOODE, Washington 174
GOODRICK, Chauncey 1511
    Wallace 1511
GOODWIN, Mr & Mrs 1133
GOODYEAR, Mr 1055
GORDEN, Alexander G 521
GORE, Mrs 511
GORGUS, Joseph W 1501
GORMAN, Charles 1514
    David 1690 Mrs 111
GORSUCH, W 945
GOULD, George A 45
    Harvey 416 Herman
    Downs 1367 Ira 885
    Samuel 106
GOUVERNEUR, Maria 744
    Samuel L 744
GOVE, Charity 986
GOWE, ALexander 315
GRACE, Capt 967
GRAHAM, David 1539
    James 1057 1215
    Sylvester 1268
    Wm 1215
GRAY, Miss 1079
GREELEY, Arthur Young
    255
GREELY, Horace 255
    Mary Y C 255
GREEN, Elizabeth 609
    James 609 John 609
    Thomas 1153
GREENBENCH, Mr 909
GREENE, Gen 619 Jane
    676 William 676
GREENFIELD, Thomas 184
GREGORY, Thomas 1191
GREIG, Mr 826
GREY, Geo 120
GRIDLEY, Henry 1074
GRIENDELL, Elizabeth 241

146

HIGBY, Wm 267
HILDRETH, M Hannibal H
    342
HILL, --- 382 1604
    Andrew 1310
    Christopher Benjamin
    1559 Eliza 464 Hiland
    914 Isaac 1083 Isaiah
    1435 Jane 464 1310
    Russell 1435 Wm 464
HILLMAN, Elizabeth M 1564
HILT, Mrs 1444
HITCHINS, Edward 546
HIXON, Hiram 1473
HOAG, Ann 1431 1589
HOBGOOD, Mr 707
HODGE, Mr 691 1219
HOES, J C F 1171 Lucas
    1130 Maria 1170 Mrs
    1171 Peter S 1171
HOGEBOOM, Tobias L 206
HOKE, David 1493
HOLDRIGE, D F 1650 Delia
    470 Robert C 470
HOLLIDAY, J 1439
HOLMES, Adeline M 1563
HOPKINS, David 832 Jane
    832 Margaret 832
HOPPING, General 1430
HORTON, Hiram 795
    Nathan 795
HOSIER, John 1569
HOUGHTAILING, John 404
    Mr 148
HOUGHTALING, James 359
HOUGHTON, John 926
HOUSE, Gerry 683
HOUSTON, Frank 1194
    James 1546 1602
HOWARD, Capt 967 Mary
    827 Mary Augusta 827
HOWE, James 358
    Margaret C 358
HOWEL, Bridget 443
HOWELL, George 885
HOWLAND, George 1503
    Jonathan 1502
HOWLETT, John 1665 1674
HOY, Julia 1572
HOYT, Capt 1673 Curtis 9
    George Washington 9
    Leger S 240

HUBBARD, Clinton 1047
HUDLER, Edgar 254 Lydia
    254 Sarah Elizabeth
    879 William 897
HUFFMAN, Nathan 298
HUGGINS, George 1417
HUGHES, Lloyd 481 Mary
    262 418 Miss 375
HUMPHREY, Charles 668
    Enos 1534 George L
    377 Henry 663
    William 377
HUMPHRIES, William 749
HUNGERFORD, Orville 1099
HUNT, Edward 1627 John
    1627 Thomas 1202
    Tilghman 1183
HUNTER, J W 88 John 1667
    Miller 1109
HUNTINGTON, Zachary 759
HUTCHINS, Thomas 100
HYATT, Mr 1391
HYLAND, William 703
HYNES, Sarah 1541
INGLES, --- 826
INMAN, Henry 842
    John 842
IRELAND, Mrs 667
IRVIN, Jesse 820
IRVING, Capt 1217
IVES, Augustus F 27
    Chauncy 27 Oscar 27
JACKSON, Andrew 789
    Henry M 641
    Joseph I 348
JAQUES, J N 294 302
JAMES, --- 452
JARNAGIN, Spencer 1192
JAYCOX, Christopher 1101
JEFFERSON, Thomas 789
JENKINS, --- 1220 Edward
    1056 Henry 1194 Mr 581
    Samuel 41
JEROME, H K 1347
    Isaac 1347
JERVER, Anthony 53
    Mary 53
JOHNSON, A 827 Chapman
    258 Charlotte 1579
    David 738 James 780
    Joseph 1494 Mr 443
    1625 Richard M 953

JOHNSON (continued)
S 638 The Prophet
715 Thomas 893
JOHNSTON, --- 618
James P 1181
JOINER, Irwin 389
JONES, Jacob 807 John
Richard 554 Major 1529
Milton 900 Samuel 1553
JORDAN, Edward 915
Mariah 516 Mary 516
Miss 1590 Selah T
516 1590
JORDON, Simon 3
JORIGAN, --- 1219
JOSELYN, Christopher 440
JOY, Andrew 176
Charles E 54
JUKENBERG, Henry 1421
JUNO, Michael 743
KASE, Mr 120
KEARNAN, Nancy 1053
KEARNEY, David 1317
John 1012 1317
KEARNON, F 288
KEARNY, General 136
John W 988 R 136
Ravaud 136
KEATOR, Harvey 1295
Lucretia 1205
KEATY, Michael 669
KEELER, John 504
KEGAN, James 419
KELLEY, Aoial 1152
Madison 908
Richard 119
KELLOGG, Epenetus 337
Maria 337
KELLY, --- 580 Daniel
1499 Thomas 1381
KELSEY, Joseph 62
KEMBLE, Woodhull 957
KENNISON, David 1401 1489
KENNY, Maria 982
KENT, Catharine 1364
Edward 995 Frederick
1020 Harriet 1020
James 1364
Mary Ophelia 1020
KERR, Robert 1705
KERRNEY, General 1430
KEYS, Thomas 793

KEYSEN, --- 188
KIERNAN, John 1039
Patrick 1508
KIERSTED, John 1294 1398
1701 Maria A 1701
KLINEFELTER, Mr 162
KILLEY, Egbert B 1433
KIMBERLY, Harvey 1448
KIMBLE, Altie 791
KINCAID, Charles 1119
KING, Ira 442
KINGSLEY, Prof 1603 1633
KINNY, Daniel 1601
KLOSTER, Maria 7
KNAPP, Benj J 1014
Elizabeth 771
Louisa C 823
KNICKERBOCKER, --- 1375
KNIGHT, --- 84 Elias 527
KNOTT, Samuel 111
KNOX, Reuben 1215
KOCHE, Jacob 1641
KRAMER, Christiana 1680
KROM, Esther 761 John
1322 Sol I 254
KROWS, Catharine 723
1250 Deborah 1305
Ellen Augusta 723
Frederick 1158 1250
1305 William 723 1250
KRUM, Isaac B 330
LACE, John M W 1706
LADD, --- 164
LAMB, Thomas 1407
LANE, Amos 388
Hardage 319
LANGDON, Joseph 1076
LANGLEY, Benjamin 1331
Phoebe 1331
LANSING, Cornelius 301
LASHER, Paul 772
LATHROP, Henry A 1237
J Greenleaf 1237
Septemus 1237
LATTEN, --- 287
LAUGHLIN, Patrick 279
LAVERTY, Patrick 932
LAWRANCE, Mr 130 Neely
261 Roswell 261
LAWRENCE, Frances Maria
336 Lewis 336 Margaret
336 Rachel 476

MATHEWS, Edward 173
  Walter 1304
MATTHEWS, Henry 364
MAUTORSTOCK, Adam 178
MAXWELL, Myles 370
MAY, Thomas C 597
MAYNARD, Elisha B 91
  Isiah 91 Jane 91
  Jeremiah 91 Rachel
  Jane 91
MAYO, Francis 1514
  Wm 298
MC ADAMS, Catharine 325
  John 324
MC BEAN, John 647
MC BRIDE, Andrew 1358
  Arthur 1358 James 1411
MC CABY, John 725
MC CAFFRAY, --- 898
MC CALL, Anthony 1557
MC CAN, James 681
  Martin 478
MC CANN, James 127
MC CARTHY, Catharine 209
  1308 E J 1702 John 208
  209 1308 Maria 1702
  Michael 194 208
MC CARTY, J 1131
MC CAW, Robert 616
MC CLUSKEY, Alice 1287
  Patrick 1287
MC CLUSKY, John 474
  William 1604
MC COBB, Ferdinand 100
  George 100
MC CORMICK, John 852
  857 899
MC COY, --- 874
MC CRACKAN, Elinor 430
MC CRACKEN, Mr 591
MC CULLOUGH, John 166
  Mr. 487 Thos 166
  William R 469
MC CUNE, John 519
MC DONALD, --- 1440
  Betsey 1053
  Charles 1471
MC DOWELL, Eliza 693
  James 1251
MC DUFFIE, George 1078
MC ELHONE, Harriet 1177
  James 1177

MC ELROY, James 558
MC EWEN, Patrick 979
MC FARLAND, Mr 98
MC GARR, Janet 167
MC GAURREN, John 584
  Mary Ann 584
MC GEE, Ebenezer 798
MC GRAPH, Barney 247
MC GREGOR, Charles 1665
  1675
MC KAY, Peter 774
MC KIEFREY, William 77
MC KINNEY, Sheriff 908
  Solomon 816
MC KINSEY, Alexand. 1193
MC KNEW, Basil 1600
MC KOWN, Geo 675
  Harriet 675 Lee L 675
MC LEAN, Andrew 1621
MC LELLAND, --- 950
MC MANNUS, --- 585
MC MILLAN, Charlotte
  1223 Donald 1223
MC MILLEN, --- 688
MC MURRAY, J 51
MC NABB, Robert 1279
MC NARNY, Arthur 1537
MC NEIL, John 579
MC NEISH, George 256
MC NULTY, Anthony 1240
  Capt 1360
MC VEAN, Charles 5
MEACHAN, Miss 263
MEAD, Harriet C 892
  Malcom W 892
MEECHAM, Thomas 508
MEEKS, Braxton 694
MELDRON, Richard T 1394
MELVIN, George 782
MENNEVAL, Baron 713
MERITT, Sarah 1221
MESSENDEN, Abraham 100
MICKLE, David 228
MIDDLETON, Mr 1112
MIER, George 119
MIKLER, Robert 1210
MILLAN, James 109
MILLER, Alpheus 615
  Benjamin F 28 Daniel
  996 Eliphalet 123
  Franklin 1158 George
  180 John Thomas 1158

MILLER (continued)
Joseph 900 Major 19
Margaret 180 Miss
1079 1369 Samuel
1219 Warren 114
Wm 119 499
MILLS, George A 1122
John J 549 T F 549
Thomas 44
MINER, Catharine H 1175
Horace 1623 Jane
Catharine Brainerd
1175 L C 1175
Mary Eliza 1623
Mennett 1623
MINSEY, John 120
MODESBURGH, H 1219
MONAHAN, John 144
MONELL, Frederick 1636
MONK, Maria 378
MONROE, President 744
MONTGOMERY, --- 1376
James 608 1303
Salina 415
MONTROSS, John Henry 1052
MOODY, Mr 1318
MOONEY, Patrick 328
MOORE, Duren 986
Elizabeth 1301 John
1301 Richd 233 Wm J 152
MORE, Eliza 250 Jacob 236
MOREHOUSE, Eben B 496
MORELAND, Mrs 1187
MOREY, Mrs 1553
MORGAN, John I 300
MORLY, John 876
MORRISON, John 756 1108
MORRISSEY, Catharine 137
MORROW, Ex Gov 1437
MOSELEY, John 399
MOULTON, Mr 318
MOUNT, Joseph 37
MULLALY, Charles 490
MULLEN, Bartholemew 690
MUMFORD, S G 859
MUNSON, Richard 726
MURPHY, Robert H 425
Taylor 1267
MURRAY, Adam 1580 J 1580
MUSE, Thomas 1016
MUSSELMAN, Isaac 523
MYER, Abm 1161

MYER (continued)
Benjamin 794 Frederick
1161 1168 Harvey 1415
J 1371 Jane 811 Levi D
1415 Peter 811 1394
Solomon 1222 Wm 836
MYERS, Jacob 733 Martha
1035 Matthew J 1515
MYNDERSE, Leah 12
MYRES, Joseph 714
MYRICK, --- 514
NANERY, James I 277
NANNERY Jas J 1172
NAPLES, King of 1163
NAPOLEON, Emperor 713
NEAL, H 567
NEALE, Dr 549
NEBARD, Jacob 1097
NELL, Jacob 537
Maria 537
NELSON, George 1434
NESBITT, George 1089
Robert 1089
NEUHOFF, Francis 46
NEWKIRK, Abram 862
Conrad 970
Philip 1176
NEWMAN, A 386
NEWTON, Miss 116
NICHOLS, Bruner 951
E A 1397 James 435
Juliet 435
William 1096
NOAH, Mordecai M 1084
NOBLE, Gen 163
NODWELL, David C 1406
Frances Emma 1406
Marian 1406
NOLAN, Matthew 468
NOLES, Jackson 1004
NOON, James 1340
William 1340
NORRIS, Andrew 1681
W C 1404
NORTON, James 1523
NOSLEY, --- 1332
O'Brien, --- 561 John
412 Major 651
O'CONNER, Thomas 601
O'CONNOR, Timothy 601
O'DONNELL, Barney 35
O'DONOGHUE, --- 1601

O'DOUGHERTY, Thos 146
O'RIELLY, Patrick 960
O'SULLIVAN, Timothy 1452
  1476
OAKLEY, James 625
ODELL, John O 340
OGSBURY, Philip 1488
OLENDERF, Levi 959
OLIVET, Jonathan S 332
OLIVIT, Hannah 332
OLMSTEAD, Polly 1302
  Samuel 1302
ONACKER, Mr 1252
OSBORN, Gideon H 87
OSTERHOUDT, A M 310
  Jacob P 310 John L 751
  Lawrence 949 Margaret
  949 Mary Elizabeth
  310 Tjerck 673
OSTRANDER, Levi 934
OTIS, Sarah 1177
  Shubael 1177
OVERBAGH, J V L 1043
  Lyman 365
OWEN, Mr 132
PADDEN, Mr 918
PAGE, Charles 394
  Samuel 1034
PALMATEER, Edward 1214
PALMER, John 746
  Orrin T 492
PARCELS, George 1145
PARDEE, Irwin 971 Mary
  Ann 156 Phineas 156
PARKER, Edward L 777
  Jonas 718
PARKMAN, Dr 828
PARKS, Mr 769 R S 743
PARSON, Geo 557
PARSONS, Mrs 781
PASQUAL, John 593
PATRIDGE, Elkanah L 1147
  Sarah Abigail 1147
PATTERSON, Abel 760
  Hannah 760 J B 503
  John A 1014 William 326
PATTON, Mr 1483
PAUL, Mrs 263 Prince 1478
PAULISON, Christian 1311
PAVOUSKY, Chas 998
PAYNE, John Howard 1513
  Woodford 1392

PEAKE, --- 662 John 840
PEARSALL, Elizabeth 1570
PEASE, Mr 1135
PECKHAM, Pardon 1282
PECORE, Mary 517
PEFFER, William 1395
PENA y PENA, 538
PENDERGAST, Charles 984
  Kate 984 Thomas 45
PENDERHURST, Lieut 686
PENNEY, Wm 600
PENNY, Samuel 600
PERKINS, Samuel 415
  Thomson 1326
PERRINE, Augustus F 369
  George 369
PERSONS, Jane 1165
  Joel 1165
PETERS, Mr 375
PETONA, Philip 402
PHEAN, Wm 763
PHELPS Abner P 1136
  Mrs 1136
PHILIPS, Anna 891
  Catharine Ann 55
  Christian F 891
  James 55 Rosina 891
PHILLIPPE, Louis 853
PHILLIPS, B T 313 John
  Jenkins 313 M E 313
  Mr 1086
PHINNEY, Henry 868
PIERCE, Benjamin 1522
  Franklin 1522
PIERSON, H P 121
PINCIN, Simeon 677
PINE, Brainerd 674 James
  S 674 Sarah M 674
PINNOCK, Abby 80
PINTO, --- 1467
PLASS, Derrick 480
  George 1351
PLATT, Jas 140
PlOUGH, Annah 1243
  Charles 1141 George
  1141 Helenah C 1243
  Jacob 1243 1378
  John 444 475
PLUMER, Ex Gov 994
  William 974
PLUMMER, Joseph 957
POE, Edgar A 429

POLK, James K 205
  President 1142
POLLOCK, Dr 319
PONDER, John G 449
PORDEN, Elenor Ann 1352
PORTER, Charles 296
  David 745
PORTNER, John Francis
  Henry 972
POST, Adam 491 Anna
  Myre 461 Isaac 502
  Israel 408 John 450
  Nelly 461 Peter 1031
  Samuel M 461
  Sarah Ann 95
POTTER, --- 843 1138
POULDING, Mr. 743
POWELL, Jeremiah 1002
  Mrs 1001
POWERS, A E 896
PRATHER, Milo 1077
PRATT, Jonathan B 716 732
PRENTISS, Henry L 520
  S S 765
PRESTON, Isaac 1549
  Samuel 1443
PRICE, John 143
PRIOR, MR 848
PROVERST, --- 906
PULLEN, Henry 602
  William T 1497
PULTZ, David I 179
PYE, Robert 1691
QUICK, Daniel S 1274
QUIGLEY, Mr 1671 Mrs
  1665 Phoebe Ann 1692
  Thomas 1692
QUINCY, Josiah 846
RADCLIFF, John 197 Mary
  345 Thos 345 W B 1432
  William Pitt 197
RAFFERTY, Michael 417
RAGSDALE, G W 657
RALEIGH, Walter 936
RAMSAY, Adam A 1338
RAMSBOTTOM, --- 84
RAND, Thos 611
RANKEN, Robert 501
RANSOM, --- 1200
  James 1436
RANTOUL, Robert 1605
RATTO, Antonio 35

RAY, Abby Ann 1571
  Caroline 1571 Wm 1571
RAYNOR, MATTHEW 1631
REDDING, --- 1680
REDDY, Bridget 1356
  John 1356
REDFEARN, John 1235
REDMOND, Phiilo 482
REED, James 76
  Margaret 76
REID, --- 1005
REILEY, Lawrence 1375
RENO, Samuel 1131
REUBEN, --- 1359
REYNOLDS, Arthur C 543
  Captain 1389 John 773
RHINEHEART, Francis 329
RHODES, Elisha H 274
  Erasmus 360 James 274
RICE, George 498
RICH, Riley 356
RICHARDS, --- 230
  A 1289 John 522 Mrs
  1270 Richard 548
RICHARDSON, Amer 594
  Elizabeth 1524 James
  223 John 956 Judge 692
  Lovina 594
RICHELLO, Mr 639
RICHMOND, Abner H 321
  Adelaide Elvireta 321
  Electa 321
RIDER, Briggs 1039
  Jairus B 1129 Mary 221
RIGHTMYER, Anna 604
  Eli 1059 Ellen 1059
  Pauline 1059 Wm 604
RIKERT, Margaret 808
RILEIGH, Hugh 1652
RILEY, Edward 305
  Rosa 305
RING, Michael 468
RIOFFREY, Bureaud 922
RISTON, William 269
ROACH, John 1530 Mr 660
ROBBINS, Uzza 873
ROBERTS, --- 15 Benjamin
  471 George 162 Mr 540
ROBERTSON, Charles 466
ROBINSON, A 1578 Abigail
  1427 Isaac D W 434
  Isabella 1578 M M 734

153

ROBINSON (continued)
Mary A 1578 Mrs 507
ROBWIN, Mr 1131
ROBY, Capt 743
ROESSLE, Jane 859
ROGERS, David 563
Jeremiah 563 Peter 483
ROLAND, Major 1697
ROMER, David 1143 1230
ROMEYN, Herman M 652 672
ROOSA, Catharine 133
Eliza 1044 Emanuel
1424 Henry 1115 Hiram
784 Lamira E 784
Norman Suydam 1044
Peter 1044
Rufus Palen 784
ROOT, --- 715
ROSA, Hyman 1206
Rebecca 1206
ROSE, James 593
ROSS, Charles 72 David
207 1148 1432 John 207
ROTE, Matthias 1555
ROULEY, John 200
ROWE, Ferdinand 452
Henry 467
ROWLAND, David 375
ROWLEY, James 1468
ROYAL, John 275 Mrs 275
RUDOLF, Hemke 46
RUGGLES, Chas I 424
RUMFELDT, John G 1649
RUMPH, John W 819
RUSH, John 901
RUSSELL, Andrew 1286
Chas 1118 Elizabeth
1019 Garrit E 374
Henry S 1342 Nancy M
1342 Nicholas 1341
1342 Peter 1019 Susan
1019 William L 889
RUST, John B 650
Philo N 1100
RUSTIN, Lydiaette 323
Richard 323
RUTLAND, Gen 17
RUTLEGE, John 215
RYAN, John 640 Martin 109
SALPAGH, Alexander 654
SAMUELS, John 1224

SAMUELS, Margaret 1224
SANCEY, Henry 997
SANDS, George H 67
Isaac 1561 1587
R A 1561
SANFORD, Judge 1588
SANGER, Captain 927
SAVOY, Dennis 1645 John
1644 Solomon 1643
SAWYER, William 1505
SCHARR, John 816
Theobald 816
SCHEPMOES, Andrew E 413
Caroline 135 Elsey 413
John R 125 135 Sarah E
413 William E 812
SCHERMERHORN, Lizzie 835
SCHIDEL, --- 1543
SCHINLEY, Capt 894
SCHONEMAN, --- 821
SCHOONMAKER, Dorcas 1259
Francis 1011 George P
571 J S 1590 Magdelena
1335 Thomas 685
SCHOTEN, Mr 1228
SCHUNEMAN, Wilhelmus
1046
SCHUSTER, Louis 729
Lydia Maria 729
SCHWARZ, Hermann 246
SCHWARZENBERG, Prince
1466
SCOFIELD, Melissa A 637
William 637
SCOT, Mr 111
SCOTT, A N 420 Charles
W 913 Gen 1619
Winifeld 1527
SEAMAN, Jo 46
SEASE, Howard 1409
SECORD, Hannah 849
SEELOFF, Carl F 1481
SEERS, Robert 1304
SELLECK, Wm 886
SELLERS, John 1435
SELTZER, Mr 816
SERAPHINA, Sister 984
SERGEANT, John 925
SEVIER, Ambrose H 11
SEWARD, Moses H 1592
Mr 1050

SEYMORE, Frederick 822
SEYMOUR, Lewis, 372
SHAFER, Simon 93
SHAFFER, Caroline 355
  Charles W 355
  Emilie 355
SHANNON, --- 1610
SHARP, Martin 199
  Peter G 271
SHARPLESS, Aaron 910
  Phoeba 910
SHAW, Benjamin 757
  Francis Augusta 954
SHEAN, Wm 762
SHEARIN, Francis 979
SHEE, Martin Archer 854
SHELDON, Dr 1283
SHELLY, --- 1485
SHENEMAN, --- 821
SHEPARD, Dyer, 1373
  Wm 957
SHEPERD, Miss 1093
SHEPHERDSON, Mr 1003
SHEPPARD, Wm 1004
SHERWOOD, Samuel 1367
SHILLING, Frederick 1533
SHIRTLIFF, Elizabeth 827
  Robert 827
SHOLTUS, John 398
SHOOK, Ira 758
SHORT, Angeline 154
SHRINER, John 128 Wm 128
SHUB, Peter B 220
SHUBERT, Stephen 265
SHUFELT, Levi 1000
SIBLEY, Mark H 1686
SIEBER, Madame 1333
SIGNER, Catharine 292
  Jacob I 292
SILSBEE, Nathaniel 778
SIMMONS, Caroline C 322
  352 353 Charlotte A
  1185 Emma 322 J W 1587
  John 322 352 353
  Mrs 1587 W H 1185
SIMPSON, William A 1258
SIMSON, James 445
SINCLAIR, James 203
SINGLETON, Mr 1112
  R W 938 Richard 1078
SINNET, George 42
SISUM, Elizabeth M 334

SISUM, George W H 334
  John Aaron, 334
SIXSMITH, John 703
SKINNER, John S 1081
  Miss 1608 T S 1372
SLACK, --- 187 702 1349
  John 393
SLOAN, Joseph 1194
SLOUGHTER, Edward 473
SMAFTZ, Mary 506
SMALLEY, Mrs 263
SMITH, Amy 35 Ann 689
  Anna Maria 1519
  Archilbald M C 1361
  Caesar 155 Charles
  407 458 Charlotte D
  493 Elisha 277 1172
  Fanny Ellen 155
  Francis Marion 1519
  Gardiner 229 George
  792 Hubert 1343
  Hugh 792 792
  James H 656 John 245
  1486 1509 Josiah 1519
  Lodowick 219 Margaret
  792 793 Mary Ann 849
  Miss 1079 1604 Nelly
  219 Solomon A 493
  William 980 Woodson 97
SNELL, Wm H 1662
SNELLING, Caroline 103
  Elizabeth 102 103
  John 102 103 William
  2 3 102
SNOOK, Reynolds 61
SNOW, Herman 688
SNYDER, --- 1248 C A
  472 Edmund 1436 Jacob
  A 1345 Paul 1694
  Vina 1436
SOUTHARD, John 1629
SPEED, J J 1586
SPENCER, Albert 885
  Allen 1091 George
  1065 Joseph 578
  Thomas 1145 Wm 600
SPENDLEY, Richard 1490
  William 1490
SPINGER, August 165
SPRINGSTEEL, Samuel 1469
STAHL, Frederick 432
STARK, Gen 44

155

STARR, --- 606
STEINGRAVER, --- 1402
STERNS, Capt 1514
STEVENSON, Capt 1622
  Edward 1521 Evan 1521
  T 51
STEWART, Charles 420
  1007
STICKNEY, Mr 565
STODDARD, S Wyman 1630
STONE, William Leete
  350
STORM, A G 985
  Edward C 985
STORY, Adam 547
STOTT, Robert 451
STOUT, Catherine 433
  E S 433
STRAIN, Jas B 244
STREET, Mrs 151 W P 151
STICKLAND, Samuel 926
STRONG, A 1098
STULL, J 1219
STYKER, Barnt W 151
STYLES, Benjamin 724
  Hannah 724 Samuel 724
SUDDERLY, Francis 1425
  Marriett 1425
  Sarah 1425
SULLIVAN, --- 839 1491
  Ellen 1350
  Jeremiah 1073
SULSER, John 82
SUMNER, Henry 790
SUMTER, General 619
SUN, Reuben 119
SUTERMEISTER, Hermania A
  1290 J H 1290
SUTTON, John 1056
SWART, Benjamin 327
  Catharine 1370 1453
  Chauncy M 1370 1453
  Eugene L 1453
  Theresa Jane 1370
SWARTHOUT, Caroline 1032
  Nicholas 1032
SWIFT, Thatcher 227
SWINDEN, Mrs 1054
SYBIL, Francis 244
SYMONDS, Cyrus W 850
TABER, Paul T 1412
TABOR, A 1412

TALCOTT, Parsons 29
TALLMAN, John B 728
  Mary Newman 728
TALLY, Mr 1292
TAPPAN, Wm B 218
TAPPEN, James C 1234
TATE, Mr 1093
TAUCALIN, --- 1610
TAUKWANG, --- 710
TAYLOR, Catharine 624
  Cornelius 457 General
  789 1430 1614 George
  624 James 530 Mr 1689
  Zachary 768 783
TEARS, Andrew 590
TEERPENNING, Samuel 50
TEETSEL, Hannah 75
TEETSELL, John 75
TEN BROECK, Henry 878
TEN BROUCK, Jane Cath-
  erine 665 Wessel 665
TERWILLIGER, Edward 902
THAYER, Charles 1506
THIELMAN, Geo 1582
THOMAS, David 749
  John 56 Mrs 56
THOMPSON, David 663 1140
  Edward 788 Elmore 1587
  Eugene 1568 George 1140
  1321 Gertrude 1321
  Jabez P 1599 John 48
  941 1568 Margaret 1140
  Maria 1336 Mary 1568
  Nancy 525 Sheldon 1072
  William 144 1336
THOMPSON, Capt 1422
THROP, Wm 433
THROWER, Laurania 283
THURSTON, Wm 138
TILGHMAN, John 1186
  Joseph J 1186
TILLUM, Mr 743
TINCKON, Wm 743
TINUM, William 1152
TITUS, Angevine 798
TODD, Samuel 1442
TOLAND, Andrew 127
  Joseph 681
TOMPKINS, Francis 655
TONER, --- 523
TOSLEY, W W 1148
TOURTELOT, Abraham 776

156

TOWNSEND, John 456
  Joseph 172 Martin 456
  Nancy 172
TRACEY, Lydia Jane 320
TRACY, Edward D 68
TRALEY, Mr 743
TRAVER, Milton J 963
TRAVERS, Philip 260
TREMPER, Aghtie 1139
  John 1139
TREMPPER, Theodore F 595
TREVANA, Juan E 99
TRIVETT, James 348
  Sarah Jane 348
TROLLER, Mr 99
TRUE, Mrs 1298 Wm 1298
TRUEMAN, John 162
TRUESDELL, M H 316
TUCKERMAN, Fanny 1396
  Joseph 1396
TURLEY, Judge 1189
TURNER, Joseph 202
  Mr 396
TYLER, James 955
  Robert 126
TYNAN, Patrick 217
TYSDELL, William H 1049
TYSON, A 379
UNDERHILL, Robert 236
VAIL, Isaac 42 Jacob 43
VALCOTT, Peter 66
VALDES, Francisco 1704
  Idelfonso 1704
VALLET, Benj F 1426
VALLEY, Francis 1405
VAN AKEN, Elizabeth 698
  Henry 698
VAN ALLEN, Archibald 406
  Catherine 406
VAN BERGEN, Anthony 1504
VAN BRAMER, Sarah 22
  Thomas 22
VAN BUREN, Mr 1133
  William 1379
VAN CAMPEN, Moses M 448
VAN DEUSEN, Emily H 1285
  George N 1285
VAN DYCK, Henry 1596
VAN ETTEN, Albert 1103
VAN GAASBEEK, Christopher
  357 Sarah 947
VAN KEUREN, Thomas 625

VAN KLEECK, Isaiah 799
VAN RENSSELAER, Solomon
  1474
VAN SANTVOORD, C 383
  William Stephens 383
VAN SCHAICK, Abm 346 347
VAN STEENBERGH Abm T 182
  Joanna 1245
  John 182 368
VAN SYLE, Nelson 161
VAN WINKLE, Judge 531
  618 Louisa C 823
VANCOURT, Alexander 284
VANDEMARK, Ann Eliza 701
  John 701 Sarah E 701
VANDERLYN, John 1695
  Nicholas 134
VANDEWATER, Peter 115
VANKIRK, Richard C 1273
VANWAGENEN, Jacob 978
  Thomas 978
VAHSAW, John 314
VAUGHAN, Charles R 234
VERBEYST, Mr 509
VERDUGO, Judan 1349
VERGNOL, Mr 160
VERNAL, Charles 863
VERNOOY, Jacob 978
VICKERY, --- 1041
VIEL, L 1066
VINCENT, --- 1219
VON BECK, Catharine 1167
VOORHEES, Ann Maria 212
  Francis C 212 Inez 212
VORUS, Hiram 542
VOSBURGH, Isaac 867
  Miss 1133
VREDDENBERG, Orrin 687
VREDENBURGH, Amelia 1693
WADE, Joseph W 799
WADSWORTH, Alexander S
  1107 M 1573
  Matilda 1590
WAGGONER, Christian 154
WAIDER, --- 1543
WAKELY, Charles 73
WALBRIDGE, Mrs 489
WALKER, Dr 840 Mrs 69
  William 940 958
WALL, John 1439
WALLACE, Patrick 708
WALLINGFORD, Wm T 586

157

WILSON, Thaddeus D 248   ZILLER, Edward 1661
   William 717 Wright 707 ZIMMERMAN, Conrad 131
WILTSIE, John 331
   Susannah 331
WINNE, Patrick 1340
WINSLOW, Abby C 1330
   Isaac 1330 Theodore
   Barrel 1330
WINSOR, John 1211
WISE, Henry A 925
   John 338 William 50
WISNER, Miss 1390
WITCHER, Merrill 72
WITHERS, Reuben 543
WOLFE, --- 1374 Gen 42
WOLFER, George Francis
   1167 Jno Andrew 1167
WOLVEN, Catharine 1306
   Elizabeth 1306
   Samuel F 1306
WOOD, James 1344
   Joshua B 1397 Matthew
   272 Tileston 1502
WOODBECK, Joel 1678
WOODEN, Henry 1255
WOODLAND, Mr 908
WOODRUFF, Ann 803 Anna
   S 1010, Elias 1158
   James 803 1010
   John 1158
WOODWARD, Dr 1284
   Judge 534
WOOL, James 1632
WOOLF, Mr 1549
WOOTEN, Dr 814
WORTH, General 1430
   Major General 169
WORTHINGTON, Mr 582
WRIGHT, J L 797 Silas 829
WYCKOFF, Mr 273
WYGANT, Lewis 787
WYNKOOP, Evert 664
   Hezekiah 791 John L 1
   Maria 626 Mariette
   664 Tobias 626
WYNN, James 195
YATES, Hiram 1552
YORK, Elizabeth 401
YOUNG, Capt 120, Daniel
   1121 John 1472 Maria
   Louisa 1121 Miss 827
   Mr 1480 Samuel 943

www.ingramcontent.com/pod-product-compliance
Lightning Source LLC
Chambersburg PA
CBHW072251270326
41930CB00010B/2347